BUILD

"Stuart Lamont approaches everything in life with raw authenticity, and his meat-and-potatoes writing style reflects this. In BUILD, Stuart combines relatable stories and metaphors with solid Biblical teaching, which will equip readers to make their own lives unshakeable. I can't wait for book two."

—Kary Oberbrunner
Chief Igniter, *Igniting Souls*
Author of *Elixir Project* and *Your Secret Name*

"Stuart Lamont draws in the reader with precious true stories from his own life. His vulnerability is real, raw, and honest. Every story ties back to Biblical principles with an emphasis on application. As you read this, you will truly meet the author—a man that Jesus built."

—Joan Turley
Author of *Sacred Work in Secular Places*

"BUILD is a timely work, reminiscent of classic writers of the past, including Tozer, Bounds, and others. The author Stuart Lamont tells powerful stories of how God worked in His life to mature him. Stuart calls to hurting people of God who are like sheep on a cliff edge, and ushers them back to safety. I am looking forward to the impact and shift this message will certainly bring."

—Martyn Wood
Empowerment Coach, *Deeper Path Coaching*

"BUILD shows the reader that spiritual success is not how good you look on the outside, but Who is living on the inside. You will be encouraged to develop a deep, vital relationship with God that makes you unshakeable."

—Eric Eaton
Author of *The Thrival Guide*, and *The Raging Sloth*

"In life, we often overthink how to achieve spiritual growth. Stuart has melded together his story, the Bible's story, and our story, to show us how to overcome the very things that hold us back. BUILD is a book for everyone seeking to create a better life for themselves, and for those around them."

—Mary Valloni
Author of *Fundraising Freedom*

BUILD

THE FOUR-STEP BLUEPRINT FOR AN UNSHAKEABLE LIFE

STUART LAMONT

Build: The Four-Step Blueprint for an Unshakeable Life
Copyright © 2018 by Stuart G. Lamont.
All rights reserved.

Paperback: ISBN 978-1-64085-186-3
Hardback: ISBN 978-1-64085-187-0
E-book: ISBN 978-1-64085-188-7

Library of Congress Control Number: 2017919511
Author Academy Elite, Powell, OH

Published by Author Academy Elite
P.O. Box 43, Powell, OH 43065
United States of America

Edited by Teri Capshaw
Author Photography by David Beach
Cover Art by mr.clutch
Interior Design by JETLAUNCH

All rights reserved. No part of this publication may be reproduced, stored in a retrieval system, or transmitted in any form or by any means—for example, electronic, photocopy, recording—without the prior written permission of the publisher. The only exception is brief quotations for review purposes.

The author has tried to recreate events, locales, and conversations from his memories of them. In order to maintain the anonymity of individuals in this book, the author has changed the names of individuals and places in some instances. The author may also have changed some identifying characteristics and details such as physical properties, occupations and places of residence.

Although the author and publisher have made every effort to ensure that the information in this book was correct at press time, the author and publisher do not assume and hereby disclaim any liability to any party for any loss, damage, or disruption caused by errors or omissions, whether such errors or omissions result from negligence, accident, or any other cause.

Scripture quotations marked NIV are taken from the Holy Bible, New International Version®, NIV®. Copyright © 1973, 1978, 1984, 2011 by Biblica, Inc.™ Used by permission of Zondervan. All rights reserved worldwide. www.zondervan.com The "NIV" and "New International Version" are trademarks registered in the United States Patent and Trademark Office by Biblica, Inc.™ Scripture quotations marked MSG are taken from The Message. Copyright © 1993, 1994, 1995, 1996, 2000, 2001, 2002. Used by permission of NavPress Publishing Group. Scripture quotations marked ESV are taken from the ESV® Bible (The Holy Bible, English Standard Version®), copyright © 2001 by Crossway, a publishing ministry of Good News Publishers. Used by permission. All rights reserved. Scripture quotations marked KJV are taken from The Authorized (King James) Version. Rights in the Authorized Version in the United Kingdom are vested in the Crown. Reproduced by permission of the Crown's patentee, Cambridge University Press. Scripture quotations marked NLT are taken from the Holy Bible, New Living Translation, copyright ©1996, 2004, 2007, 2013, 2015 by Tyndale House Foundation. Used by permission of Tyndale House Publishers, Inc., Carol Stream, Illinois 60188. All rights reserved.

For Rachel.
You taught me that His perfect love casts out fear.

TABLE OF CONTENTS

Note to the Reader xiii
Foreword xv
Introduction xix

Part 1 – Push
The Will to Win

Chapter 1 – The Wake-Up Call. 3
Connect with Reality and Invite God In

Chapter 2 – What Do You Want?. 11
Set a Course for Transformation

Chapter 3 – The Cycle of Spiritual Growth 21
Get with the Program

Chapter 4 – Why Grow?. 29
Decide to Go Deeper

Part 2 – Position
Set Up to Win

Chapter 5 – The Paradigm Shift 43
   Respond to God's Gift

Chapter 6 – Are You a Good Person? 53
   Come as You Truly Are

Chapter 7 – Sonship 63
   Experience God as "Father"

Chapter 8 – God is With You 73
   Listen to God the Holy Spirit

Part 3 – People
Together We Win

Chapter 9 – Shared Success 85
   Take People with You

Chapter 10 – Let God PICK 97
   Connect with the Right People

Chapter 11 – For Different Seasons and Different
Reasons 107
   Look to God as Your Source

Chapter 12 – Don't Be a Stranger 115
   Be a Friend

TABLE OF CONTENTS

Part 4 – Programming
Thinking to Win

Chapter 13 – Chasing Fantasy 125
   Embrace Reality with God

Chapter 14 – Zeal Without Knowledge 135
   Get Acquainted with God

Chapter 15 – The Unsealed Letter 145
   Trust Him at All Times

Chapter 16 – The City Gates. 159
   Guard Your Heart

Conclusion – Our Enemy Trembles 167
Appendix – Believing in Jesus 171
Acknowledgements 175
About the Author 181
Notes 183

NOTE TO THE READER

It is significant that you have picked up this book. The principles we will discuss together have the power to radically transform your life.

Each chapter ends with a section called "Building Blocks," which are the chapter's key takeaways. I encourage you to spend some time reflecting on these points to reinforce what you are learning.

If you wish to dive deeper into the subject of spiritual growth, the "Notes" section at the back of the book will provide opportunities for further reading.

Get ready to BUILD.

FOREWORD

Stuart first joined *Life Unlimited Church* when he was fifteen years old. He came to us, emotionally bruised and unsure of himself. Our youth leaders rallied around him, loved him, and did life with him. Before long, Stuart developed a love for the Bible. God started to heal him inside. Stuart became active in our church and served for five years in our worship team.

Stuart now has a wife and two daughters. It is not rare to see Stuart looking after his daughters at the back of our evening service, releasing his wife as she sings and leads in the worship team. Stuart is an invested Dad and a supportive husband.

Similarly, ever since I became a Christian as a teenager, I loved the Bible. Through all kinds of difficulties, including my time as an operational medic in the army, I grew closer to God and drew great strength and wisdom from the Scriptures. Now as a pastor, I have made it my mission to teach others what God has revealed to me through His Word. I know God's Word is the truth, and as people engage with Jesus and embrace God's Word in their lives, they are transformed and set free.

Without being paranoid, I know that spiritual opposition against God's people is very real:

> "For our struggle is not against flesh and blood, but against the rulers, against the authorities, against the powers of this dark world and against the spiritual forces of evil in the heavenly realms."[1]

This means that a "Sunday School" level of spiritual maturity may help you get started in following Christ, but it is not enough to help you endure until the end. To stay the course in the Christian life, you need to keep growing spiritually.

BUILD will exhort you to "grow up" spiritually, so that you can be the overcomer Jesus calls and empowers you to be. You will be challenged to develop intimacy with God, realign your motives, partner with people, and renew your mind for success. You will be encouraged to see how God is interested in every detail of your life.

Sean Stanton
Senior Pastor
Life Unlimited Church
Canberra, Australia

INTRODUCTION

In the Old Testament, the prophet Elijah has a showdown with 950 enemy prophets. Elijah sets up an altar with wood and rocks and a sacrificial bull, then pours water all over it. He did the tangible things he knew to do, in order to prepare for a miracle from God. And, sure enough, when he prayed and asked God to come and receive his offering, God sent fire down on the altar and burned up everything, including the stones and the water.[2]

This is what I believe life with God is about: we position ourselves and prepare. Then He comes and does the things that we could never do ourselves. The Bible says that God can do in one day, the things that would take us a thousand years.[3] I hope you will take this opportunity to invite God into every sphere of your life. He cares about all of it. Is every sphere of your life of equal importance? No, but He still cares. Take God along for the journey.

I am no theologian, but I wrote this book as an act of obedience to God. I believe that my life's mission is to, "Meet people in the valley and take them up the mountain." Just like Elijah went up the mountain and experienced God, my prayer is that this book will help prepare you to live a life punctuated with mountain experiences—moments where you meet with God. Moments of joy in His presence.

I believe the Bible is the unique hand-print of Almighty God, harmonizes with history, and yet can speak prophetically to each of us in countless ways. God can use a passage in His Bible to speak to 100 people in 100 different ways. In light of that truth, BUILD is held together by the metaphor of Nehemiah's wall (seen in the book of Nehemiah, chapters 1 through 6). Think of the city of Jerusalem as a metaphor for your life. The city wall represents your spiritual maturity. And the gates of Jerusalem represent your discernment—your ability to choose what ideas, people, or things you allow to affect your life.

The message of this book is that spiritual maturity is not an optional extra; it is a critical component if you are going to fulfill your purpose on earth, and finish your own race.

In the developed world, there is a popular notion in church circles that once you ask Jesus to become your Lord and Savior, you are "set for life" and can go on to autopilot, living as you used to live. This is a dangerous view to embrace. When it comes to your spiritual life, you cannot afford to sit on the fence. Your spiritual life is not like deciding how many stars to give the movie you just watched. Instead, it is like a boat on the open sea; you are always moving. Either you are moving towards God, or you are moving away from Him. Jesus Himself spoke often of the importance of staying close to Him:

> Why do you call me, "Lord, Lord," and do not do what I say? As for everyone who comes to me and hears my words and puts them into practice, I will show you what they

are like. They are like a man building a house, who dug down deep and laid the foundation on rock. When a flood came, the torrent struck that house but could not shake it, because it was well built. But the one who hears my words and does not put them into practice is like a man who built a house on the ground without a foundation. The moment the torrent struck that house, it collapsed and its destruction was complete.[4]

Jesus also tells us what can happen if we do not stay close to God:

I am the vine and you are the branches. If you remain in me and I in you, you will bear much fruit. If you do not remain in me, you are like a branch that is thrown away and withers; such branches are picked up, thrown into the fire and burned.[5]

One of the telltale signs that we are drifting from God is that our love grows cold. As Jesus told His disciples:

Because of the increase of wickedness, the love of most will grow cold, but the one who stands firm to the end will be saved.[6]

You can see from the above passages that sitting on the fence is not an option. Those who belong to Christ are new creations,[7] who live in this world but no longer belong to it.[8] The gravity of this world, and the pressures of life will continually keep you on the ground, unless you push against those forces with the upward thrust of faith.

This book is divided into four sections, which cover four key components of an unshakeable life. This kind of life is one that stands firm until the end—meaning the end of your life on earth.

As we begin this journey, let me encourage you. If you are reading these words, it means you are alive, and therefore there is still hope for you. You may have been walking with Christ for five minutes, five years or five decades, but I am here to tell you that God wants you to experience more of His goodness in your life today.

This may sound wonderful, but don't be complacent. There is an enemy—the devil. His messengers will come to you and ask, "What makes you think you have authority to rebuild this wall?"[9] This is exactly what happened to an historical figure named Nehemiah, when he worked to rebuild the wall of Jerusalem. Similarly, you will face doubts that prompt you to think, "I cannot do this," or "Maybe I shouldn't try too hard to be free in Christ; what will people think?" Remember to stand firm, and keep the words of God Himself on your lips.

Before we begin, let's pray together:

"God, thank You for loving me enough to send Jesus to earth, so I could be close to You. My heart is open. I may have doubts, but I am ready for this journey. Please teach me how to be unshakeable. In Jesus' name, Amen."

PART 1

PUSH

THE WILL TO WIN

1

THE WAKE-UP CALL
CONNECT WITH REALITY AND INVITE GOD IN

That Life-Defining Moment

Do you remember where you were during spring break in the year 2000? Most people I knew—and a good portion of people around the world—were crowding around televisions to watch the Sydney Olympics unfold. I, however, was making my way to a small Australian beach town. Little did I know that a week-long camp would completely change my world.

I was about to attend a Christian camp for students. Most of us wore t-shirts, shorts and flip-flops. This was the backdrop to what, for me, would become a life-defining experience.

I turned up early to the bus rendezvous point and tentatively climbed aboard the bus. Looking around, it was clear that people knew each other. There was plenty of chatting and laughing. I was fine not diving into the conversation. I was far out of my comfort zone and hedging my bets. Then, something out of the ordinary happened. One of the leaders, a senior in high school, was standing near the front of the bus. She locked eyes with me and smiled. I went along with it and smiled back.

The next morning, I went to the food hall for breakfast and found her standing there. Jenny (not her real name) started making small talk. My mind filled with questions: *Why is this leader talking to me? Who am I?* With a long track record of rejection at the hands of my peers, kindness was unexpected.

I grew up in a stable, loving family. However, my memories of elementary school are tainted by bullying and victimization. My so-called friends would hide from me every lunchtime. I couldn't even take the hint that they didn't want me around. Despite this, I tried to convince myself that I liked school. After all, I received affirmation through the narrow field of academic achievement. My self-image was as thin and fragile as tissue paper. I thought life was unpleasant, but I deserved it. I despised myself. The fantasy life I created was more enticing than the real world. I survived by daydreaming. Meanwhile, I studied hard to earn my teachers' approval, yet rarely achieved top grades.

I doubt Jenny has any idea how much of an impact she had on my life. Over the course of that week, she took an interest in me as a person, which for me was mind-blowing. Then on the final night of the camp, one of the camp organizers gave a talk about Jesus. Afterwards, we were given time to reflect and to respond to the offer of salvation through Jesus. In a tender moment, Jenny took me aside and spoke to me about beginning a relationship with Jesus Christ. I do not remember the specifics of the conversation, but as she prayed with me, I was hit with a sense of safety like I had never experienced. Looking back, I know for a fact that I was experiencing the love of God. To me, it was a miracle.

I left that camp a different teenager. Prior to camp, I was an undiagnosed insomniac. I had to listen to the radio to get to sleep each night because the silence was deafening. Before bed, I would sit in my room, and reflect on how I had nothing to look forward to in my life.

But after camp, I experienced something new. I lay on top of my bed to process the events of the camp. Next thing I knew, it was the next morning, and I was still on top of my blankets and wearing the clothes I wore home from camp. From that day, I no longer suffered from insomnia. I had just witnessed another miracle; it was the peace of God.

Coming to the End of Yourself

At camp, I came to the end of myself. Our subconscious is potent and will do its best to keep us from reflecting on things that may be unpleasant. But the Spirit of God can infiltrate any kind of intellectual or emotional barrier. Many people who do not know Jesus will tell you that they are not sinners, nor do they feel comfortable identifying as such. I don't blame them. After all, it is too painful to suffer that kind of guilt alone. On the contrary, that day at camp when I turned my life over to Jesus, the sense of His love was stronger than the sense of my guilt. Jesus Himself tells us, "I am the gate; whoever enters through me will be saved. They will come in and go out, and find pasture."[10]

The day will come when you need to decide that you will stop trying to fix your life on your own. The Bible tells us that God can do more in *one day* than you and I could ever hope to achieve in a thousand years.[11]

Crossing Over

Experiencing salvation is like becoming a citizen of a new country. I know of a friend who lived abroad for several years.

She even changed her citizenship to her new country. In an interesting twist, she returned to her old country and married a local! She is able to stay permanently in her original country, however in legal terms, she no longer "belongs" there. There are times that life continues for my friend, as it did before. But, every time there is a democratic election, my friend cannot vote and is reminded that her citizenship is elsewhere. Similarly, if you belong to Jesus, you are a foreigner on earth.

I urge you to begin to identify with a new kingdom—God's kingdom. How? Surrender your life over to Christ right now. From that point on, you will truly no longer be of this world. Your citizenship will be in Heaven.[12] For more details about this crucial decision, please go to the Appendix at the back of this book. Make sure you seize this crucial moment!

The Report

Speaking of being a foreigner, there is a man in the Bible who knows all about that struggle. Nehemiah lived in a foreign land. His whole nation had been exiled to the kingdom of Babylon. Nehemiah himself was the cup bearer to the king of Babylon. As an exiled Jew, he longed for Jerusalem—the heart of Israel. When his brother and a group of Jews returned from a journey to Jerusalem, they shared some bad news:

> They said to me, "Those who survived the exile and are back in the province are in great trouble and disgrace. The wall of Jerusalem is broken down, and its gates have been burned with fire."[13]

Notice that the wall had been reduced to rubble, and the city gates had been burned. Over the course of this book, I will challenge you to view the wall and the gates as a metaphor for your spiritual maturity—meaning the components of your life which identify you as a Christ-follower and protect you from harm. An ancient city without walls and gates was wide open to attack, from every angle.

What is this wall made of? In my own experience:

- The right PUSH (motivation)
- The right POSITION (relationship with God)
- The right PEOPLE (divine appointments)
- The right PROGRAMMING (worldview)

In the chapters that follow, we will unpack each of these topics. I will share stories from my own life, along with truths from the Bible that have strengthened me through the storms of life.

The Realization

Let's examine Nehemiah's response to the bad report from his brother:

> When I heard these things, I sat down and wept. For some days I mourned and fasted and prayed before the God of heaven.[14]

When you are convicted of a problem in your life—meaning when God helps you see an area you need to change—always run towards God and not away from Him. This could be your need for salvation, or a problem that God reveals as you walk with Him through everyday life. Don't worry; we've all got issues. People may be involved in some form in the process of healing, but you must make the conscious choice to involve God in your life. The Spirit of God can come in and silence all the noise in your mind. You *can* experience the peace of God. But you need to be willing to work through your emotions *with* God. Give God permission to do His work in you.

The Response

After Nehemiah's realization that Jerusalem was in trouble, he made a choice which we all should make. He did not take his pain to friends, or social media. Instead, he humbled himself under the Mighty Hand of God.[15]

Nehemiah prayed, and reminded himself of God's character and promises. Then he asked God to give him success when he asked the King of Babylon for help. Let's follow the story:

> Then [Nehemiah] said:
> "Lord, the God of heaven, the great and awesome God, who keeps his covenant of love with those who love him and keep his commandments, let your ear be attentive and your eyes open to hear the prayer your servant is praying before you day and night for your servants, the people of Israel. I confess the sins we Israelites, including myself and my father's family, have committed against you . . ."
> "They are your servants and your people, whom you redeemed by your great strength and your mighty hand. Lord, let your ear be attentive to the prayer of this your servant and to the prayer of your servants who delight in revering your name. Give your servant success today by granting him favor in the presence of this man."
> [Nehemiah] was cupbearer to the king.[16]

Maybe you do not have strong visible emotions like Nehemiah did. Maybe you do not consider yourself the "emotional type." Perhaps you feel numb. Maybe you feel stuck in the status quo of dysfunction and unfulfillment. Whatever the case, choose to respond in faith—that is, choose to think and act like what God says is true.[17]

Nehemiah clearly recognizes that prayer is the best response to bad news. His prayer recorded above was raw and unscripted, and revealed some crucial points:

1) Prayer realigned his perspective on the problem.

2) Prayer allowed him to acknowledge his shortcomings and regrets.

3) Prayer helped him see the opportunity God had placed right in front of him.

Once you have humbled yourself before God, so many amazing things become possible. In the next chapter, let's set a course for transformation.

Building Blocks

- The love of Christ is far greater than the pain of your guilt.
- Prayer is the best response to "bad news."
- If you belong to Christ, you are a "new person," and your citizenship is Heaven.

2

WHAT DO YOU WANT?
SET A COURSE FOR TRANSFORMATION

When I was 11 years old, I developed unusual medical issues. First, I experienced hypersensitivity in one ear. All sound became too loud. I was already partially deaf. Then, I became dizzy if I looked at a point higher than 45° above the horizon. My issues at school went to a whole new level. I wore a brightly colored foam earplug in my only functioning ear. That resulted in almost two years of taunts, laughter, and bullying.

One day, however, everything changed. I started asking God to take these problems away. I was not eloquent, and I didn't know much about God at that age. But I decided to believe that God could fix my problem. Here is what I learned: change happens when we acknowledge our current reality and partner with God to usher in a new reality.

One morning, I woke up and realized that I didn't need to put my earplug in. On the same morning, I looked up at the white ceiling—straight up. I wasn't dizzy! Then I caught the bus to school and noticed the pattern on the ceiling of the bus for the first time in years. It was a thin wooden sheet, laminated white, and riddled with circular holes that you could fit a pencil through.

Next, I stepped into my school building and was surrounded by an intimidating group of boys from the class ahead of me. They started taunting. One said, "Let's take his earplug!" He leaned forward and looked in both my ears, one at a time, and seemed disappointed—and almost embarrassed—when he could not find the earplug. The group of boys began to file away, and all disappeared within seconds.

God is real—and He cares.

Nehemiah and the King

This same God was with Nehemiah, weeping over Jerusalem. As we saw previously, Nehemiah brought God in on his sorrow and reaffirmed that God was able to help him. Now, we are about to witness God moving in his life. Nehemiah tells the story like this:

> In the month of Nisan in the twentieth year of King Artaxerxes, when wine was brought for him, I took the wine and gave it to the king. I had not been sad in his presence before, so the king asked me, "Why does your face look so sad when you are not ill? This can be nothing but sadness of heart."
>
> I was very much afraid, but I said to the king, "May the king live forever! Why should my face not look sad when the city where my ancestors are buried lies in ruins, and its gates have been destroyed by fire?"[18]

Notice what happened next. The king asked a provocative question:

"What is it you want?"[19]

This question used to make me cringe. Not anymore. This is one of the most life-changing questions you can be asked. It is a question that brings clarity. In fact, coming to terms with what you want will make or break your quest for spiritual maturity. Nehemiah boldly responded to the king:

> Then I prayed to the God of heaven, and I answered the king, "If it pleases the king and if your servant has found favor in his sight, let him send me to the city in Judah where my ancestors are buried so that I can rebuild it."[20]

We're reading the story of a man who knew what he wanted. In fact, he was able to state his case with confidence to a foreign, heathen king. How did he get this kind of clarity?

The Perils of Not Knowing

To answer this crucial question, I'll tell you about the time I tried out the gym near my office. Everybody was "in the zone," pumping iron and hitting the treadmill. Music videos were blasting from wall-mounted TVs. I sat down with Steve, my personal trainer. He asked me, "So, what are your fitness goals?" I confidently recited my goals—to eliminate shoulder pain and reduce body fat by 5%.

Steve gave a sigh of relief, saying, "I think we'll work well together. Recently I started with two new clients. Both of them said they are seeking 'general fitness.' The proof is in the pudding. Even though they are paying tuition fees and showing up, they don't follow my instructions, and so they aren't really improving at all."

Can you see the wisdom there? Both clients at the gym were dissatisfied with their level of physical fitness, but they did not really understand what they wanted to achieve. In contrast, I had done my research and identified where I wanted to be.

How does this apply to your spiritual life? In my case, I have encountered many people whom I want to be like. Some are peaceful even in difficult situations. Some model kindness that changes the atmosphere. Others accept me in contradiction to every negative belief I held to be true regarding myself. I started to get envious (in a good way) of the traits these people exhibited. Then it dawned on me; these people are following Christ, and His character is rubbing off on them!

Friend, Jesus Christ is not only our King, but He is also our example. The Bible calls Him the Word of God.[21] He Himself is the standard—or the blueprint—for an unshakeable life. Make Him your life's goal.

Bethesda

Jesus is also the greatest at asking provocative questions. One day, Jesus visited the pool of Bethesda. The word on the street was that this pool had healing properties. Many beggars with disabilities congregated there, waiting for a lucky break. Jesus turned up and singled out a man who had been at the pool for thirty-eight years.[22]

The man participated in the same ritual day-after-day, in the hope that he would be healed. He probably had hope at the beginning. However, the story speaks of a man stuck in a rut. Until he receives a wake-up call from God Himself. John retells the story for us:

> When Jesus saw him lying there and learned that he had been in this condition for a long time, He asked him, "Do you want to get well?"[23]

If I were that beggar, I think I would have said "Yes!" After all, wasn't it obvious from the situation why he was there? Why did Jesus ask that question? I believe it was because the man had stopped hoping. Put simply; hope is a desire. The Bible tells us: "Hope deferred makes the heart sick, but a longing fulfilled is a tree of life,"[24] and, "The human spirit can endure in sickness, but a crushed spirit who can bear?"[25]

Let's look at the man's response:

"Sir," the invalid replied, "I have no one to help me into the pool when the water is stirred. While I am trying to get in, someone else goes down ahead of me."

This man had lost any reason to keep going. He was now wide awake with this question, and spoke of his isolation; no one was there to help him. Perhaps even the people around him had lost hope too.

Then Jesus said to him, "Get up! Pick up your mat and walk." At once the man was cured; he picked up his mat and walked![26]

In here lies my point: If your life is a ruin, don't stay down. Look to Jesus. Just like the man in this story, Jesus wants you to make a decision—to get up, pick up your mat, and walk.

Get Up

I truly believe that Jesus does miracles, even today, but He usually requires our cooperation. It is not a completely one-way transaction. Jesus gave the man a command to get up. Notice that the man's role in the miracle was small. At this point, the man's state of learned helplessness was shaken. Suddenly, he regained influence over his circumstances—perhaps for the first time since he was a boy. He had to stir up hope again. He had to take action.

There was a time in my life where I was praying to God to deliver me from a certain thought pattern which was causing me to feel insecure around people. After asking many times for help, God's reply one day was simply, "You are more healed than you know." I hadn't even noticed that God was healing my broken heart. This knowledge helped me to leave my comfort zone.

No matter what issues you are battling, keep partnering with God and let Him talk you into wholeness.

Pick Up Your Mat

Think of the mat as your testimony—your struggle, your circumstances, or your mistakes. The Bible says that we overcome by the blood of the lamb and by the word of our testimony.[27] I even rediscovered parts of my story through writing this book. Don't forget what God saved you from. Especially as you apply God's principles for spiritual growth. There will come a day when you may struggle to remember how your life used to be. You may find that you traded yesterday's problems for today's new challenges. Remembering how far you have come will keep you full of gratitude, and will keep you hungry for more growth.

We see the importance of remembering God's goodness in Psalm 77. At the beginning of the chapter, the writer pours out his heart before God; he feels weary and abandoned by God. Then, he changes his tune: "I will remember the deeds of the Lord; yes, I will remember your miracles of long ago."[28]

You may have heard it said that "your mess will become your message." Think of it. There are people out there whom perhaps you have not met yet, who need to hear your story and observe the way you live. What surprises me most is that you cannot always predict who you're going to help.

And Walk

Do what you could not do before—walk! Step into exciting new experiences. You may meet new people, start a new job, or venture into a new relationship. When you walk—and keep walking—you embrace the amazing things God has done for you. Keep walking, holding onto the knowledge that God is for you and not against you.[29]

Learn to acknowledge the disappointments and mistakes that may have caused your bondage. Mourn them if you have to. Then, approach God with the expectation that your tomorrow will be better than your today, and your yesterday.

Much of life with God is "walking with God." Notice that we tend not to say "run" with God. Why? Life is not meant to be a rollercoaster. We are not designed to be frantic all the time. We need peace and rest. You need to play the long game. Your time on earth is more limited than you may think. Prioritize your relationship with God, and don't be afraid to stick with that decision. It will count for eternity.

Motivation that Transforms

As we delve deeper into the message of this book, take a moment to ponder your motivation for wanting to improve your life. There are three "paths of motivation" you can choose to take. The first path is the path of pleasing others—acting to ensure that you have the approval of your family, friends, co-workers, passers-by, or people on the Internet. The second path is pleasing yourself. This path is shared by people who feel they are done trying to please others (and those who never cared that much about what others thought to start with). Both of these paths will lead to an undesirable destination.

As you continue to engage with this book, my prayer is that you would embrace the third path—the path of pleasing God. As the Apostle Paul wrote, "No one serving as a soldier gets entangled in civilian affairs, but rather tries to please his commanding officer."[30] In the same way, fix your eyes on pleasing the only One Whose opinion truly matters. This path does not always provide warm-and-fuzzy feelings, but it will sustain you. It will take you where, deep down, you truly want to be. If pleasing God is your core motivation, then you are on the path to healing, restoration, blessing, fulfilment, and longevity.

Play the long game.

Building Blocks

- Faith is about doing the small part of the miracle and relying on God to do the big part.

- Until you prioritize faith over feelings, you will have no power to change.

- A motivation to please God first will lead to an unshakeable life.

3

THE CYCLE OF SPIRITUAL GROWTH
GET WITH THE PROGRAM

God Was There

During my university years, I was fortunate enough to spend ten months in Japan as an exchange student. This opportunity was a dream come true for me as a twenty-year-old. I love Japan. I encountered amazing sights, delicious food, and friendly people. I found an incredible local church and grew a lot in that environment. My Japanese was sufficient to understand my classes, but the cultural learning curve was steep. My aversion to *nomikai* (drinking parties) meant that I missed out on many chances to mingle. I found myself not connecting with other international students.

Living alone for the first time was challenging. I had frequent conflicts with a difficult person—myself. Constrained by misguided self-beliefs, I drove myself further into isolation.

There were even a few days where I did not speak to another human being—except perhaps the local convenience store clerk. I would go to the store, pick up a ready-made *bento* (lunchbox) and take it to the counter. The clerk would ask, "Would you like me to warm up your lunch in the microwave?" I would aptly respond, "Yes, please." Apart from that formulaic exchange, my only company was me, myself, and I.

It is one thing to be uncomfortable with other people, but what if you are uncomfortable with yourself? This experience forced me to learn how to accept myself. It was intense, yet one of the most valuable and formative experiences of my life. That trip is still paying emotional and spiritual dividends for me today.

Toward the end of my time in Japan, I made a discovery: I could not only look at my face in the mirror, but I could get up close to my reflection and stare myself down! Not only had my endurance level increased by several notches, but I had developed the character to accept myself. God had a plan to help me grow, and He has a plan for you too.

The Four Stages

Walking with God is a slow-and-steady journey. It can be easy to grow tired, weary, and discouraged. These symptoms do not necessarily mean you are off-track.

The Apostle Paul tells us about the importance of difficult times ("sufferings"):

> And we boast in the hope of the glory of God. Not only so, but we also glory in our sufferings, because we know that suffering produces perseverance; perseverance, character; and character, hope. And hope does not put us to shame,

because God's love has been poured out into our hearts through the Holy Spirit, who has been given to us.[31]

Paul touches on what I call *the Cycle of Spiritual Growth*. There are four stages of the cycle, and you can think of them as seasons. They invariably follow each other in sequence. Let's examine them, one by one. They are:

- Suffering
- Perseverance
- Character
- Hope

Suffering

Amazingly, Paul tells us that we ought to "glory" (or rejoice) in our sufferings. Was he warped? Not at all. There is something about experiencing pain that can make us stronger. In fact, we are told that even Jesus learned obedience through suffering.[32] While the form and severity of distress may vary from person to person, this step is essential. Pain is an inescapable part of life on earth. If you never experienced pain, how would you ever know if anything is wrong?

Perseverance

Picture someone going to a gym to lift weights. Lifting a specific weight may be challenging for a time, but eventually, the body adjusts to the weight, and it becomes too easy. Human muscles only grow when pushed to their limit, and there is a degree of pain and discomfort. This is also true spiritually. You cannot build your "muscles" without resistance. God has greater things for you ahead, and so He needs you to keep getting stronger. Some people say that we go through trials, so that we can learn to be more grateful. This may be a by-product, but it is not the whole picture. God is not just a two-dimensional, paper God. He is three-dimensional, and He pays attention to every area of your development as a person. His goal is to make you more effective in His kingdom, and a better advertisement for Him to a broken world. Persevere with a good attitude, and people will take notice.

Character

Your character is your baseline-of-behavior—or your 'B.O.B.' for short. This is how you behave when nobody is watching. People can try to work on their character apart from God, but usually, this results in bondage. It ultimately creates new problems. Instead, let God do His work in you to make you more like Him. After all, He is the potter, and you are the clay.[33]

Some of you may have learned to drive in a car with manual transmission. Driving is hard enough with all the things you need to be aware of: road rules, speed limits, pedestrians—and, of course, other vehicles! Many people these days shy away from learning to drive a manual car and choose an automatic transmission instead.

For someone who has just started driving with manual transmission, it can be sensory overload. There is so much to think about. Changing gears can be tricky. But what happens when you have been driving for six-to-twelve months? Shifting gears and operating the pedals become second nature. You don't have to think about them anymore.

Friend, this is what character is like. Character is your automatic response to a situation, regardless of whether anyone is watching. God is full of wisdom, and so be grateful that He will not promote you until the right time.[34] You cannot go to a new level of blessing, influence, or calling until you pass the character test. Before you move on to a new trial, God wants to see that your automatic response is to do the right thing. He is your promoter, not people. He is a good Father, and He is committed to helping His children grow in humility and character.

Hope

There is no experience like realizing one day that your character has been upgraded. God does His work on your character in such a way that there is no doubt in your mind that He did it. He rightly deserves all the credit. When you experience a breakthrough like this, you will be energized. What's more, your God-given dreams will be a step closer to fruition. Don't give up. There's a payoff if you stay in the game. Remember what the Apostle Paul says:

> Let us not become weary in doing good, for at the proper time we will reap a harvest if we do not give up.[35]

Paul ends his powerful commentary on the Cycle of Spiritual Growth with these words:

> And hope does not put us to shame, because God's love has been poured out into our hearts through the Holy Spirit, who has been given to us.[36]

We must go through sufferings, develop perseverance, and establish character. Then we are reminded of the hope we have. As we just saw in Scripture, God pours His love into our hearts by the Holy Spirit. The bottom line is this: The cycle of spiritual growth will help you to build a deeper understanding of God's love.

Do you realize how much God loves you? This is the Biblical worldview: As followers of Christ, we know that God loves us no matter what, because of what Christ did for us on the cross. There may be trials in your life, but this does not nullify God's love. Choose to worship and honor Him in the midst of your difficulty. This will result in some of the most powerful experiences of God's love.

No Shortcuts

Listening to people preaching the word of God is an integral part of growing as a believer, but know this: there are no shortcuts to spiritual growth. The people that are at the front of the room preaching or teaching have gone through their own process. Don't be surprised if at times applying what someone else has done in their life does not work for you "as-is."

The Apostle Paul tells us to work out our salvation "with fear and trembling."[37] This fear is not a negative dreading of God, but rather a reverence for God. There is no more important activity in this world than growing up in God. Take this seriously. Make time for it in your schedule. Value it more highly than overtime, even more than social events. Your relationship with God is precious, and so is your spiritual growth. No one else can do this for you. You need to invest in your spiritual life.

You need to play the part of a scientist. Be a person who relentlessly seeks the truth. It is said that Thomas Edison, the famous inventor, made hundreds of light bulb prototypes before he came up with a design that worked. Don't be afraid of a little trial and error. As long as you keep spending regular time in the Word of God—the Bible—you will find that your spiritual "ears" will be tuned to hear God's voice directing you.

Pray that God would bring to you an accountability partner—someone who can encourage you, but also can tell you the truth when you most need to hear it. Regular feedback is an invaluable part of your growth. Without honest feedback, you will start to minimize, or even overlook your own shortcomings. Continue along this path for long enough, and you may even tolerate your own destructive attitudes or behaviors. This is a dangerous place to go.

When Your Strength Fails You

I found myself in a hospital recently. My ankle was swollen, and I didn't know why. It turns out I had just rolled my ankle. What a relief. This is a common ailment, but I didn't even recognize it. After all, I never played sports much growing up.

The doctor decided to immobilize my ankle with a small cast. What the nurse didn't tell me is that the cast was going to warm up my leg. Long story short, I started to sweat profusely and then I passed out. I woke up to the doctor holding my face with both hands, and several people standing over me. (That would have to be my scariest medical story! What's yours? Oh, actually it's okay not to tell. This is a book, so I can't hear you anyway!)

I learned something from this experience: by far the best place in the world to lose consciousness is in a hospital. Why? Because the people there are both able and willing to help. Similarly, where is the best place to be when your strength fails you—when you are going through tough times? It's in the presence of God. How can you meet with God? You can encounter Him one-on-one, and in a grace-filled Bible-believing community of Christ-followers.

My encouragement to you? Don't quit. The journey may be difficult, but keep leaning on God more and more.

Building Blocks

- Spiritual growth is not a linear process. It comes in cycles, and you may deal with an issue multiple times.

- Character is your automatic response to a situation, regardless of whether anyone is watching.

- The best place to be when your strength fails you is in the presence of God.

4

WHY GROW?
DECIDE TO GO DEEPER

The Band-Aid Principle

I have two beautiful little girls. At the time of this writing, both recently started school. When they were toddlers, one thing that perplexed me was my children's obsession with band-aids—those universally-loved plastic strips for covering cuts and abrasions. They are available with all kinds of cool patterns, whether it is a famous black-and-white mouse, a silver-haired princess who lives in an ice castle, or just about any character with a cape. They come in all sizes too, though the adult-sized ones tend not to be as decorative. (Note to self: this might be a good business venture!)

Apart from the fashion appeal of band-aids, there is a mystery that I like to call "the band-aid principle." You see, my children have a strong mental association between *band-aids* and *healing*. Isn't it interesting that a band-aid does not actually have healing properties? It is a hygiene product which protects broken or exposed skin from contamination and infection. Yet my children used to always ask me for a band-aid, even when there was no injury requiring treatment!

My daughters also used to practice sympathetic band-aid wearing—the technical term. If one daughter cut herself and "earned" a band-aid, the other would insist to the point of tears for a band-aid of her own. I would say, "No, you don't need one," but she would persist until she got one anyway!

Children can teach us so much about ourselves. After all, even if you are an adult, you are just a "big child." (No offense.) Your human condition and basic motivations have not changed all that much. Hopefully, by now, you have gained self-control, forbearance, and a sense of responsibility. But there may be ways in which you still live by the band-aid principle as an adult.

You see, band-aids have the following characteristics, represented by the acronym SKIN:

1) They are **Superficial**

   The effectiveness of band-aids is only skin-deep. Band-aids are a means of addressing surface injuries. A band-aid wouldn't help much in treating a broken arm.

2) They **Keep** falling off

   Band-aids tend to come off at the most inappropriate times. You need to carry spares to keep those wounds covered.

3) They do not prevent further **Injury**.

   We put band-aids on after children hurt themselves—not before. Personally, I don't cover my children's knees with band-aids each morning "just in case." (If I did, I would probably give them bike helmets too.)

4) They are a **Nuisance!**

> There is only one way to remove a band-aid—quickly! Don't prolong that burning pain of pulling skin and hair. To remove my children's band-aids, I first have to shield myself from their cute tiny flying fists. In some ways, this is worse than never having a band-aid in the first place!

My point? You need to decide if you are going to settle for "surface healing" for your soul, or whether you want to deal with your real issues. As silly an example as band-aids may be, the principle is the same. Superficial solutions will deceive you. They will keep letting you down, and you will likely get hurt again. In fact, you will probably end up worse off than you were before. Do yourself a favor: commit to grow spiritually and get closer to God.

Your Choice

We know that spiritual growth helps us experience the love of God more deeply and increase our capacity to know and serve God, and it happens in cycles. Still, the question remains: What is the impact of choosing *not* to grow spiritually?

The Apostle Peter came across some Christ-followers who needed to renew their pursuit of God. This is what he told them:

> [God's] divine power has given us everything we need for a godly life through our knowledge of him who called us by his own glory and goodness. Through these he has given us his very great and precious promises, so that through them you may participate in the divine nature, having escaped the corruption in the world caused by evil desires.
>
> For this very reason, make every effort to add to your faith goodness; and to goodness, knowledge; and to

knowledge, self-control; and to self-control, perseverance; and to perseverance, godliness; and to godliness, mutual affection; and to mutual affection, love. For if you possess these qualities in increasing measure, they will keep you from being ineffective and unproductive in your knowledge of our Lord Jesus Christ. But whoever does not have them is nearsighted and blind, forgetting that they have been cleansed from their past sins.[38]

Peter agrees here with the Apostle Paul about the Cycle of Spiritual Growth, but Peter goes a step further to offer the reader two choices: keep growing or backslide. There is no such thing as "standing still" in his definition.

Peter knows what he's talking about.

Don't forget that this is the same Peter who went through an amazingly authentic process of growth. In the Gospel of John, we see Peter (a.k.a. Simon) transform from a timid, impulsive and carnal person, to the leader of the early church.

The first thing Jesus did when He met Simon was to change his name.[39] Simon's new name—Peter—means "rock" in Greek. In the beginning, he kept trying to run ahead of Jesus, and even tell Him what to do! Imagine having the audacity to tell God what to do! (I am sure I have done this at some point. What about you?) When Jesus was going to the cross, Peter made a vow that he would never abandon Jesus, but he did. Then he labeled himself a failure and went back to what he was most comfortable with—his fishing boat. But Jesus found Peter and extended forgiveness to him.[40]

Do you feel like you have failed? Don't worry. Peter thought his journey with Jesus was over. In fact, he went back where he started—on a fishing boat, only to see Jesus there! If Jesus can forgive Peter—who denied that he even knew Jesus—then He can forgive you. Don't give up. Get up. Try again.

Keep Your Creator on Your Calendar

Just like an athlete that does training all-year-round, even when they are not competing, so we need to be consistent. This does not mean that you will always be able to spend the same amount of time with God in your devotional time. Nor does it mean you will always volunteer the same amount at church. What it does mean is that God is still on your speed-dial, whether you are in a good season or a bad one. In fact, the Apostle Paul wrote to his protégé Timothy and instructed him to "be prepared in season and out of season."[41]

What happens to athletes who stop training for a long period, start watching television, and eating potato chips five hours a day? They will soon start losing their muscle tone, and they may even put on some weight. In the same way, you owe it to yourself to keep your Creator on your calendar, and do what you can to keep that vital relationship alive.

Naturally speaking, spending time with God does not present any direct economic benefit, and so there doesn't seem to be a tangible return. In our modern world, we are conditioned from a young age to think about making money. In fact, if you look at most people's motivation for doing things in the developed world, whether it be study or work, it is fair to say that most people do these things in the hope of making money. But what if I told you that spending time with God will profit you more than paid work? I am talking about the God who is capable of meeting your every need. He exhorts us to give our anxieties to Him because He cares for us deeply.[42] If you invest more time each day getting to know your Creator, you might not feel the need to self-medicate with TV, social media, food, or anything else that offers a quick fix.

Stay in the Game

It is commonly held that goldfish can swim around the same fish tank day after day for months on end, because they have an incredibly short-term memory. One day, on TV I saw a cartoon goldfish in a fishbowl. There was a small castle in the water. The goldfish would go about its routine. Every time it completed a revolution and saw the castle, it would exclaim, "Oh look! A castle!" Again. And again.

This is perhaps not a flattering comparison, but you and I are like goldfish—well, at least in spiritual terms. Why do I say this? If you have been following Jesus for any length of time, it is very easy to forget, or at least lose sight of, basic truth. How about the fact that you are saved by grace alone and not by your own merits? What about the fact that you are a more than a conqueror through Christ?

It is time to break free of spiritual amnesia. This brings me to an all-important passage in the Bible that is perhaps well-worn, yet severely under-applied. Romans Chapter 12 says, "Therefore, I urge you, brothers, in view of God's mercy, to offer your bodies as living sacrifices, holy and pleasing to God—this is your true and proper worship. Do not conform to the pattern of this world, but be transformed by the renewing of your mind. Then you will be able to test and approve what God's will is—his good, pleasing and perfect will."[43]

Even after you get saved, your mind would still be full of all the stuff that was in there before. It doesn't just disappear into thin air. You need to retrain your brain gradually over time, just as you would retrain a muscle. To retrain your brain, you must model the right behaviour consistently. Again. And again.

Now, popular teaching would dictate that this requires you to obsess over rules and regulations. That is simply not true. It is good to know and abide by Godly principles. But instead, use your energy to remember Jesus Himself. In the book of Ecclesiastes, the writer says, "remember your Creator in the days of your youth."[44] At the Last Supper, Jesus commanded His disciples to practice communion in remembrance of Him. The criminal that was crucified next to Jesus addressed Him, saying:

> "Jesus, remember me when you come into your kingdom." Jesus answered him, "Truly I tell you, today you will be with me in paradise."[45]

What about the electric lights in most houses? To the naked eye, they appear to be always on. This is an optical illusion. The electrical supply to the lights actually oscillates—or flickers—fifty to sixty times per second. Electricity is used up as quickly as it comes. Without the constant supply of energy, the light will go out. Be consistent. Just like the bridesmaids who kept their lamps burning while waiting for the bridegroom as in one of Jesus's parables, so we must always be ready.[46]

How then do we live in a way where our spiritual life keeps growing all the time? Here are a few ideas:

- Try to set aside even just 15 minutes a day to spend with God, and read His Word.

- Commit to attending a church gathering, at minimum three times a month.

- Sign up for a course about spiritual growth, such as *Alpha*.[47]

The Power of Review

Journaling is another powerful way to continue growing spiritually. When you keep a journal and start writing out your prayers to God, you clarify your thoughts. It also lets you look back and see how God has done things in your life, and you can tangibly see the results of your prayers.

The book of Proverbs tells us:

> The wisdom of the prudent is to give thought to their ways, but the folly of fools is deception.[48]

If you are anything like me, as you were growing up, the importance of hard work was instilled in you. With a potent cocktail of pressure and deadlines, you learned how to work hard and long. But notice this: even God had rest. When God was creating the world, He rested on the seventh day. Was this because He was tired? No. The Bible teaches that God "will neither slumber nor sleep."[49] I believe rather that God models the power of review for us. Giving thought to our ways is more than just focusing on the task at hand. If we never review our lives, then how can we ever hope to improve and grow? We will continue doing the same things, day in and day out.

Many years ago, I was at a church conference, and singer/songwriter Paul Baloche imparted a powerful technique for spiritual growth. It was simply to keep a journal. Since then, I have filled stacks of journals. Looking back, sometimes I rambled about what I did that day, but I gained amazing clarity about my life. I credit that one piece of advice for a significant portion of the spiritual growth that I enjoy today. If you take nothing else away from this chapter, start journaling. It will change your life. You cannot overcome a problem that you cannot verbalize.

My formula for journaling is very simple. I might spend a few sentences describing what happened to me that day, but then I might pull out something that I'm thankful for, excited about, or perhaps something unpleasant that happened. At times, this is just my thoughts straight onto the page. But other times, it can be a prayer directly to God. There are no rules, other than the ones that you make for this.

Just experiment, and find something that suits you. At the end of the day, this needs to be something that you learn to enjoy abundantly and practice almost every day. I say *almost* every day because there are always those certain days that fall outside your normal routine. But whenever you do have a routine day, make sure you take time to review.

There is another key benefit of journaling. You can see how God is changing you. It is very encouraging to remember how God has looked after you in the past. I have journal entries where I have been so excited about what God is doing in my life that I've written them completely in capital letters! I believe that you will have this experience too if you commit to the process of spiritual growth.

My Challenge to You

As you continue to read this book, you will get the most out of it if you have a clear mind. The best way to get a clear mind is to set aside time every day to journal. It is amazing how much you can achieve in just 10 minutes of journaling. This habit also has an unexpected benefit. The more you write about the things of God, the more you think about them. God Himself begins to take up real estate in your mind. When He moves in, there is less room for rogue thoughts from last night's TV drama, or the mistake you made at work yesterday. When you're driving, on the train, or on the bus, your mind begins to gravitate to the things of God. Those hard questions that you haven't been able to answer, begin to come to the surface. You naturally want to talk to God more, ask Him questions, and simply hang out with Him.

Building Blocks

- Stop settling for superficial healing, and set a course for transformation.

- People forget easily; that's why we need to renew our minds daily.

- If you do not take the time to reflect on your life and God's place in it, you are too busy.

PART 2
POSITION
SET UP TO WIN

5

THE PARADIGM SHIFT
RESPOND TO GOD'S GIFT

The Problem

It seems I had a knowledge gap.

At school, I always saw a mysterious, circular, ticking clock on the wall, in every room. My peers in the fourth grade could point at the clock and say, "It's two o'clock!" I was dumbfounded. How is it that they could read an analog clock and I couldn't? After all, I could read a digital clock, and that made perfect sense. Years later, however, I had a light-bulb moment and came to understand the reason why I could not read an analog clock.

When I was in the third grade, my family spent a year in the United States. When I arrived in the States, I had almost finished the third grade already, because the Australian school year starts six months earlier—in February instead of August. My new American school decided not to take a risk, and they made me repeat the third grade. To make matters worse, I moved to another US city six months later and went straight into the fourth grade. Then, another six months later, I moved back to Australia and skipped to the end of fourth grade. To this day, I am convinced that the analog clock was taught during those six months of elementary school that I never completed. It is embarrassing to admit that I could not read an analog clock confidently until I graduated from high school.

This was a somewhat humorous setback to have had, but what is not-so-humorous is the fact that too many Christ-followers have a crucial piece missing from their belief system as well. Every wall needs a strong foundation. Before you go any further on our journey together, let's ensure our foundation in Christ is firmly laid. Without Christ at the foundation, the wall of maturity you build may look good, but it will eventually crumble. If you fail to understand what Jesus Christ has done for you on the cross, and how this applies to your life, you will unconsciously search for fulfillment (and a sense of self-worth) from other things in life.

I think we have all experienced the tyranny of guilt and shame. One day you might feel like you can take on the world, and the next day, for whatever reason, you feel like crawling into a hole. I have two pieces of good news for you. First, you are not alone in this, and, second, Jesus has overcome guilt and shame. In fact, Jesus has overcome sin and death.

I am guessing you may have heard the Good News by now, but just to quickly recap: It is by grace that you have been saved through the sacrificial death and resurrection of Jesus Christ, our God-made-flesh.[50] But salvation is more than just an event or a point in time: I am here to tell you that grace is something you must stand within.[51] This is what I call *Positional Righteousness*. It is the idea that you are not made righteous by your own deeds, but by standing "in Christ." It is about trusting completely in Him.

THE PARADIGM SHIFT

In the Bible, the writer of the book of Hebrews laments the lack of understanding his readers had regarding what Jesus had done.

Here is how it is put in The Message translation:

> I have a lot more to say about this, but it is hard to get it across to you since you've picked up this bad habit of not listening. By this time you ought to be teachers yourselves, yet here I find you need someone to sit down with you and go over the basics on God again, starting from square one—baby's milk, when you should have been on solid food long ago! Milk is for beginners, inexperienced in God's ways; solid food is for the mature, who have some practice in telling right from wrong.[52]

Can you see what the writer did there? He or she called the audience out as being a bunch of "babies." Nobody likes that. I sure don't. What does the writer mean? The bottom line is this: When anyone first meets Christ, he or she starts out as a spiritual "baby." Just like physical babies, these new believers are learning the ropes and usually receive a lot of input from God and more mature believers to encourage them to grow. I have two children, and it made sense that they started out life wearing diapers. That's perfectly normal. What if, though, they are still in diapers when they reach twenty years old? Their lack of independence would probably not be cute anymore! In the same way, it is important that you do not stay a baby Christian, but rather make a decision that you will take ownership of your spiritual life, and ultimately do what it takes to grow up. The writer of Hebrews continues:

> So come on, let's leave the preschool fingerpainting exercises on Christ and get on with the grand work of art. Grow up in Christ. The basic foundational truths are in place: turning your back on "salvation by self-help" and

turning in trust toward God; baptismal instructions; laying on of hands; resurrection of the dead; eternal judgment. God helping us, we'll stay true to all that. But there's so much more. Let's get on with it![53]

You can read this book, become more informed, and encouraged by its message and even get fired up. You can be inspired to build relationships, serve in your local church, or even take a step of faith with your career. But, if you do not build your life and service to others on the foundation of Positional Righteousness, you will end up disappointed.

You may see results for a while, and might even help a lot of people, but as soon as you become weary or offended, watch as the cracks begin to show in the structure you are diligently building. And the cycle will repeat itself. Things go well, something goes wrong, and then you lose your passion. Trust me—I know. For many years I lived by the approval (or disapproval) of others—both real and perceived—and not by God's approval.

There's an expression that I hear people use when they want to get promoted at work, and this is to "climb the corporate ladder." There is nothing wrong with hard work and self-improvement, but can you apply the same logic to your relationship with God? No! Because a relationship with God is a gift that only He can give. In the same way, don't walk into church and try to "climb the Christian ladder"—namely doing things merely to be popular with the "right people." If you have the heart to serve, then serve, but do it because you know that God already accepts you. By all means, serve others, not to gain approval from God or people, but rather to celebrate the ultimate price that God has already paid for you. The work Christ did for you is finished, and there is nothing you can add to it.

The Two Paradigms

Now let's discuss what I call "The Two Paradigms." Put simply; a paradigm is a way of thinking—a "worldview." The paradigm that you depend on will determine your results in life—and ultimately—your destiny.

The World's Paradigm

Think of this paradigm like a see-saw. On one end of the see-saw is rebellion. People at this end of the see-saw do whatever "feels right." These people might believe that being righteous is too hard, so they don't even bother trying.

On the other end of the see-saw is compliance. People at this end take heed of God's commands in the Bible, they may even attend multiple church services per week, volunteer, and donate money to mission organizations. They may even have visible leadership roles in church and be well-thought of. All these things are good, but spend any length of time with these people, and you will sense that something is missing.

There are also plenty of people in the middle of the see-saw. These people generally view themselves as good people, and they "live-and-let-live." There are those who even reject the idea of "organized religion" and feel content not having any spiritual accountability.

You may notice the implication that even "good people" can do plenty of good works and still be operating under the world's paradigm. Do I have your attention?

It may seem more obvious that people who outwardly rebel against God may have a problem on their hands, but why am I grouping them with a significant number of people who are doing "above-average" morally or even "okay"? Let's explore God's Paradigm and examine the contrast.

God's Paradigm

Unlike the World's Paradigm, God's Paradigm is not about what a person does or does not do. Instead, God is evaluating people on their faith response to Jesus Christ. Either they accept Him as Lord, or they reject Him. If you have any doubt at all about your relationship with Jesus, please read the Appendix at the back of this book.

The implications of this paradigm are huge. To unpack this great truth, let's turn back to Genesis and explore the story of Abram (later known as Abraham):

> ... Abram said [to God], "You have given me no children; so a servant in my household will be my heir." Then the word of the LORD came to him: "This man will not be your heir, but a son who is your own flesh and blood will be your heir." [God] took [Abram] outside and said, "Look up at the sky and count the stars—if indeed you can count them." Then he said to him, "So shall your offspring be."
>
> Abram believed the LORD, and [the LORD] credited it to him as righteousness.[54]

Right here, God promises the aging Abram that he will have more descendants than he can count. This requires a miracle because Abram has no children. But understand this: when God speaks, it changes us. The mark of God's paradigm is that through it we trust in His ability and not our own.

As we can see in the book of Romans, Abram set a precedent for all of us that put our faith in Christ for our salvation:

> If, in fact, Abraham was justified by works, he had something to boast about—but not before God. What does Scripture say? "Abraham believed God, and it was credited to him as righteousness."

> Now to the one who works, wages are not credited as a gift but as an obligation. However, to the one who does not work but trusts God who justifies the ungodly, their faith is credited as righteousness.[55]

This is a far cry from the world's paradigm, where people boast in either their moral merits or in their rebellion. In God's Paradigm, Jesus has done the work of justifying you and I. We simply need to put our trust in Him.

The Shift Takes Time

Because you will need to unlearn one paradigm to learn another, this process will take time. God knew that Abram would take time to apply the new paradigm to his life. God worked with Abram for a period, and He allowed Abram to grow in understanding of God's paradigm. Abram was far from perfect. He was a three-dimensional character with fears and doubts, just like you and me. Fortunately for us, the Bible is candid about his mistakes.

At one point, Abram was worried that he would be killed by the Egyptian king because of his beautiful wife, Sarai. Abram pretended to be Sarai's brother to save his own skin. Sure enough, Sarai was soon taken away to the king's harem. I can't help but wonder how Sarai felt about this situation![56]

Later on, Abram tried to bring about God's promise of offspring by his own strength. He grew impatient and went to have a child with his wife's maid—without consulting God at all. The Apostle Paul explains that this first child (Ishmael) represents our dead works—when we get fed up waiting for God to do something in our lives, and we try to make it happen without Him.[57]

I am so glad that God is patient with us. About thirteen years after the birth of Ishmael, God revisited His promise to Abram. First, He changed Abram's name to Abraham—a name that means the "father of many nations."

Then, God changed Sarai's name to Sarah and declared that Sarah would have a child at the age of ninety. This was going to take a miracle. In fact, Sarah laughed at the (im)possibility. When you come to the end of yourself, and you have no more methods with which to solve a problem, then God Himself can freely get involved in your situation and do a miracle. God strategically uses miracles to reveal Himself to His people—whether they are physical, spiritual, mental, emotional or financial. Be prepared for Him to bring any miracle He wants, by any method He wants.

What This Means for Your Life

It is not insignificant that the child born to Sarah and Abraham was called Isaac—meaning "laughter." God wants to give you something to laugh about, but you need to give up trying to make things happen on your own, and instead walk closely with Him and listen to His voice.

You may be asking right now—what does Abram trusting God for a promise have to do with my salvation? That is probably because you are more comfortable with the World's Paradigm. Sadly, too many Christ-followers trust in Christ for their salvation at the beginning, but then they keep living by the World's Paradigm. After all, this makes logical sense to them, and their emotions are even wired that way.

To make the Paradigm Shift successfully, you must renew your mind with God's Word:

> So here's what I want you to do, God helping you: Take your everyday, ordinary life—your sleeping, eating, going-to-work, and walking-around life—and place it before God as an offering. Embracing what God does for you is the best thing you can do for him. Don't become so

well-adjusted to your culture that you fit into it without even thinking. Instead, fix your attention on God. You'll be changed from the inside out. Readily recognize what he wants from you, and quickly respond to it. Unlike the culture around you, always dragging you down to its level of immaturity, God brings the best out of you, develops well-formed maturity in you.[58]

What else do you need to know about Positional Righteousness? We will keep unpacking this concept in the coming chapters.

Building Blocks

- Understanding the grace of God is not merely "nice-to-have"—it is critical.

- Your standing with God is determined by your response to Jesus Christ. Is He your Master?

- Renew your mind with God's Word daily, and you will stay dependent on His grace.

6

ARE YOU A GOOD PERSON?
COME AS YOU TRULY ARE

My Story

As a boy, I liked to point out when others had broken the rules. In fact, one of my first report cards at school put it diplomatically, "Stuart has a strong sense of justice." I was blind to the times when I had even worse blunders myself. I was also an expert on the problems of bystanders and passers-by. Then one day, things changed. I met a girl.

Like with most romances, there were plenty of warm-and-fuzzy feelings. Before long, gears shifted, things became serious, and friction began to build. The way that she and I did everyday things were worlds apart—even on the micro level. We found ourselves almost constantly offending each other—not on purpose, of course.

We ended up getting married. I confess I kept causing trouble in our relationship. You see, I had a closely-held belief that I was more morally upright than my wife. Yep. Once I came to this realization, I found the freedom, not just to say "sorry," but to *prove* I was sorry by changing my behavior.

I had this view that if others were offended by me, it was their problem. This was an ill-conceived survival technique that I had to unlearn. In her school days, my wife was more likely to sit at the back of the class and talk with her friends. Meanwhile, I used to sit at the front and be a "good boy." Then one day, God showed me that behind my rule-keeping, front-of-the-class, "teacher's pet"-type persona, I was a sinner. My standing before God was no better than that of my wife. After all, there is only one way we could both be forgiven and made right with God. It is through the perfect sacrifice of Jesus Christ on the cross for us.

A Society of "Good People"

Most of us think of ourselves as being good people. After all, we pay our taxes, we try to control our temper when we're driving (well, most of us), and maybe we even volunteer with a church or charity.

Here's the thing: regardless of how good you think you are, you need a Savior. The Bible tells us that "all have sinned and fall short of the glory of God."[59] Some people think they can make it through life on their own. Well, guess what? This life is only a dress-rehearsal for the real thing—eternity. Don't be deceived: you will reap what you sow. The Bible teaches us that Jesus Christ is the Son of the Living God,[60] and there is no other name that can save us from eternal death.[61]

The Key

When I first got my driver's license, I drove a little car called the Daihatsu Charade. It was a small, boxy, yellow hatchback straight out of the 1980s. You see, that was in an era when central locking was uncommon. One day, I drove to a fast food joint. I stopped in the parking lot, pushed the lock button, got out of the car and shut the door. Then, I had a sinking feeling. The car keys were still in the ignition. Sheepishly, I had to call my Dad to rescue me—and the car.

From that time on, I resolved to always use the key to lock the car door. Think about that for a second. The key is the method by which I access my car. By their very nature, keys are exclusive. There is only one type of key that can open my car. In the same way, faith is like a key. To what? To grace and goodness beyond what we deserve. The Apostle Paul tells us that we access grace through faith.[62] So how does one become a "good person"? It's not through good deeds or being born in a "good family." Instead, it is by trusting in Jesus to make you right with God.

Jesus is your substitute. The Apostle Paul tells us:

> … God put the wrong on him [Jesus] who never did anything wrong, so we could be put right with God.[63]

This is out of God's great love for you that He sent Jesus to die in your place.[64]

Elsewhere, Paul writes:

> If you declare with your mouth, "Jesus is Lord," and believe in your heart that God raised him from the dead, you will be saved.[65]

If people perceive themselves as being morally superior to others, we say that they are "self-righteous." Think about that. It's an oxymoron. "Self" and "righteous" do not go together. We can see from the passage above that only Jesus can make you right with God.

This is awesome news for you. If you look at any of the people God chose to work through in the Bible, you will see that most of them had something not-so-good happening in their character. Abraham lied.[66] Jacob deceived.[67] Moses murdered.[68] David killed one of his top soldiers so he could have the man's wife![69]

Good News

Fortunately for you and me, God already knows our dirt. If that was your main excuse for not going to the feet of Jesus and giving your life to Him, then what's left? By the way, God accepting you as you are because of Jesus is not just something that happens when you first meet Jesus. God continues to accept you as you are, even as you start to behave better, which is a natural outcome of walking with Jesus. Don't forget where you came from. As we discussed in an earlier chapter, don't forget that once upon a time, your walls were broken down, and your gates were burned. Don't forget that if you have given your life to Jesus, you have "passed from death to life."[70] This is not an insignificant, external change in your lifestyle. This is a change to the very core of your being.

You may be asking, what is the point in doing good works if I am already accepted by God? Well, to begin with, when you start walking with God, His very nature rubs off on you. Think of when you were a child. I remember a friend, who used to talk like a three-year-old, even though he was seven or eight. I eventually started copying him, and one day, my mother told me to cut it out. Don't be fooled. The people that you spend the most time with will influence your thinking, your beliefs, and ultimately your destiny.

Meanwhile, let's not forget the words of James, the brother of Jesus:

> What good is it, my brothers and sisters, if someone claims to have faith but has no deeds? Can such faith save them? Suppose a brother or sister is without clothes and daily food. If one of you says to them, "Go in peace; keep warm

and well fed," but does nothing about their physical needs, what good is it? In the same way, faith by itself, if it is not accompanied by action, is dead.[71]

Remember: what you do is still important, but your position before God is pivotal. You must have your identity in Christ. Then your deeds will align with your new identity. Otherwise, you will end up frustrated, and, eventually, you will drift away from God.

In my twenty-something years walking with Jesus, I have had the experience multiple times, where I settle. This is never a conscious thing, mind you, this is me beginning to get puffed up and comfortable. One of the things that inspires me the most about Nehemiah's life is his willingness to leave everything behind to rebuild.

If we look at the story of Nehemiah as being the story of your life, maybe you also have this feeling that something in your life is not right. It may be an emotional hurt, it may be your physical health, or it may be that you do not walk with Jesus at all. Whatever that "badness" may be, I encourage you to face it together with the Lord Jesus Christ. He died a lonely painful death on the cross of Calvary, to give you eternal life.

Don't even settle for "good enough." Once things in your life start improving, and you start to experience freedom, you may think to yourself, "This is all there is." If so, you are selling yourself short. While it is fantastic to be grateful for how far you've come so far, past success can also rob you of future victory. Jesus is the true measure of what your life can be. When you spend time in the Bible, which is the Word of God, you will see grace and truth. Truth shows how you fall short, but grace gives you the power to be more like Jesus. And I am not only talking about your character. God cares about the whole of you—your physical body, your finances—in a way where there is no detail missed.

There was a gentleman at our church who used to speak at the men's group from time to time. To my surprise, he approached me one night, and asked, "If you don't mind me asking, why is it that you are always so happy?" After a moment of pondering, I replied, "Because I believe that God is interested in every area of my life." I believe that answer did not come from my intellect, but it came from God Himself. It was too clear to be me—and I know me.

When you let Jesus be your righteousness, you will see the world differently. Stop trying to earn approval from God, your friend, an authority figure, or even yourself. Let Jesus be your righteousness. You will see the world differently—and you will start to experience God's love pouring into you like warm soup.

"This Is My Son"

As mentioned earlier, I have a profound hearing impairment. When I was about five years old, I had a perfect hearing test, but a few weeks later, I was in bed with a high fever. Nerve damage rendered my right ear virtually useless. For more than two decades I have experienced a world without *stereo*. I tend not to pay top-dollar for headphones. What's the point? I can only hear out of one side anyway. Surround sound? To me, it just seems, well, *louder* than normal sound. I don't see what all the fuss is about. At parties, I struggle to hear conversations. I tend to either completely dominate the conversation or opt out altogether. After all, I am the most comfortable when I can hear the person speaking—it may as well be me. On the flipside, opting out usually means I go home early, or sit next to the table and graze on party food for hours.

I have asked God many times over the years to reverse this damage. After all, He has the power to raise the dead—healing ears can't be too hard. I still believe He can do it. But His response to me one day stopped me in my tracks: "Stuart, you need to learn how to listen."

Over at least two decades living with this hearing impairment, I learned something: listening has very little to do with your physical ears. Listening is a heart issue. In order to listen to others, and receive what they say, we need to humble ourselves enough to stop talking and focus on the person speaking.

Simon Peter was a friend of Jesus and traveled with Him for years. Peter is a forerunner for us today. He is credited with multiple firsts in the early church, including walking on water. But the Bible reveals he was rough around the edges—a lot like me, and you, if we're humble enough to admit it. His successes and failings are recorded for our encouragement.

In Matthew, Chapter 17, we see Peter go with Jesus up a mountain and watch a supernatural event (known in church circles as "the transfiguration"). Let's pick up the story in verse 1:

> After six days Jesus took with him Peter, James and John the brother of James, and led them up a high mountain by themselves. There he was transfigured before them. His face shone like the sun, and his clothes became as white as the light. Just then there appeared before them Moses and Elijah, talking with Jesus. Peter said to Jesus, "Lord, it is good for us to be here. If you wish, I will put up three shelters—one for you, one for Moses and one for Elijah."[72]

I am not a theologian, but Peter's words here look like filler to me. He is known in church circles as being an impulsive character who often jumped the gun and said things he maybe should not have said. I know that many times my preoccupation with "being heard" by others can get in the way, especially in my relationship with Jesus. In fact, we live in a connected world where social media allows people to share their opinions and views with anyone, as soon as the thought hits the mind, without even a nod to self-control.

Fortunately, God interrupted Peter's monologue and gave us a powerful principle:

> While he was still speaking, a bright cloud covered them, and a voice from the cloud said, "This is my Son, whom I love; with him I am well pleased. Listen to him!"[73]

There you have it. If you only get a single takeaway from this entire book, make it this one: The secret to winning on planet earth is to value the words of Jesus above the words of anyone else. Period.

This may be a scary thought for you. You may have come to believe that God doesn't like you—that He is merely tolerating you, or is still mad at you for something you have done or failed to do. These ideas do not come from Jesus, but from the devil—the enemy of your soul. Do not listen to that broken record.

Look at what Jesus did next:

> When the disciples heard this, they fell facedown to the ground, terrified. But Jesus came and touched them. "Get up," he said. "don't be afraid."[74]

Jesus is the same person today as He was that day. You may be terrified. You may be emotionally bankrupt. You may be broken. But Jesus wants to say to you, "Get up; don't be afraid." If you trust in Jesus today for your salvation, then He will forgive all your sin—past, present, and future. If you would like to make this decision now, please jump to the Appendix at the back of the book.

As we move on, I am reminded of what my dear wife says: "Don't use your strength to make things happen in your life;

instead, use all your strength to believe in Jesus." Be brave. Make Him your "Number One" today.

Building Blocks

- Rather than be self-righteous, invite Jesus to make you right with God.

- Faith is trusting God to do something on your behalf. Faith is the key to accessing God's grace.

- Jesus wants to come alongside you and say, "Get up; don't be afraid."

7

SONSHIP
EXPERIENCE GOD AS "FATHER"

Adopted as Sons and Daughters

There are so many books out there about self-help. These gurus who write these books show people how to be a "better version of themselves." The advice they give may seem perfectly valid. But, at the end of the day, that person does not know you. You might buy a course, a book, or attend a conference. This is a business deal. One of the key differences between "self-help" and "God-help" is that God wants to adopt you as His own. He wants you to carry His name. A public figure is human and has limits, but God is limitless.

The Apostle Paul talks about God being a Father:

> For those who are led by the Spirit of God are the children of God. The Spirit you received does not make you slaves, so that you live in fear again; rather, the Spirit you received

brought about your adoption to sonship. And by him we cry, 'Abba, Father.' The Spirit himself testifies with our spirit that we are God's children. Now if we are children, then we are heirs—heirs of God and co-heirs with Christ, if indeed we share in his sufferings in order that we may also share in his glory.[75]

No Father Can Compare

Jesus bought you with a price. If He didn't value you, He never would have gone to the cross for you. Not only have you become righteous and blameless through Christ, but you also have been adopted into the Family of God. God is your Heavenly Father.

The thought of God being a Father may not mean much to you, or it may even invoke pain. It is often said that your perception of your earthly father has a profound influence on how you perceive God the Father. Your father may have been warm, affectionate, reliable and attentive, or he may have been cold, distant, haphazard, and indifferent. Perhaps your father was a blend of the two ends of the spectrum, or perhaps your father has never been a part of your life.

Be encouraged that God is a perfect Father. He is the best Father any of us could ever hope for. Let's explore how God is a superior Father to the one you knew (or never knew) through the acronym GRACE. Why grace? Grace is intrinsic to God's character.

Let's explore the acronym:

- **G**ood
- **R**edemptive
- **A**ttentive
- **C**onsistent
- **E**nduring

Good

It may seem obvious that God is good, but we should not skip over this point. How can you trust someone whom you know does not have your best interests at heart? In the passage below, Jesus contrasted the people's thinking with God's thinking:

> "Which of you fathers, if your son asks for a fish, will give him a snake instead? Or if he asks for an egg, will give him a scorpion? If you then, though you are evil, know how to give good gifts to your children, how much more will your Father in heaven give the Holy Spirit to those who ask him!"[76]

Jesus just told His listeners that they are evil. Evil is a strong word. Yet we can see from other sayings of Jesus in the Bible that He often uses such polarizing language to emphasize His point. Another such example is when He tells his disciples that they should "hate" their own families. We can see from here that the word "hate" is merely a device for emphasis. In context, it means that we are to love Jesus far more than anyone else in our lives.

We can take great solace in the fact that God's intentions toward us are good. The Prophet Jeremiah reminds us that God has a good plan for our lives:

> "For I know the plans I have for you," declares the LORD, "plans to prosper you and not to harm you, plans to give you hope and a future."[77]

Redemptive

God the Father desires to redeem you—to take you in as His own. In the Psalms, David boldly declares:

> Though my father and mother forsake me, the Lord will receive me.[78]

I believe that no parent sets out to deliberately do a bad job. This also rings true for anyone else that steps in to raise or mentor a child. The child bonds to these authority figures and trusts them like no-one else. Get this: even if the most important people in your life abandon you—even if it is your own parents—God promises to receive you and be your "perfect parent." He can love you like nobody else can. Today as you are reading this, you may be broken down like Jerusalem's city wall, but God has a plan to restore you to better than new.

Attentive

God the Father is watching you and cares about the details of your life. David writes:

> Before a word is on my tongue you, Lord, know it completely.[79]

You and I were born with a deep desire to know and be known. Guess what? God made you to be relational. If you feel lonely, do not give into the thoughts of self-doubt that you are somehow not worth knowing. Loneliness is like being "hungry" for companionship. It is God's way to point us toward connection. Start with God. You won't regret it.

Consistent

God the Father never changes. The Apostle Paul penned these words:

> Every good and perfect gift is from above, coming down from the Father of the heavenly lights, who does not change like shifting shadows.[80]

One of the wonderful things about God is that He never changes. No matter what day of the week it is, whether the sun is shining or hail is falling, whether you just climbed the heights of success or the bottom has just fallen out of your life, God is the same. He is not moody. He does not have sugar highs, hangovers or hayfever. He is ever-dependable and ever-strong. Consistency is part of His guarantee to you. This means you never need to ask God, "Is now a good time?" Simply approach Him. His office door is always open. In fact, He is expecting you.

Enduring

God the Father never quits. As Paul sought to encourage the church in the city of Corinth, he encouraged them by reminding them of God's faithfulness:

> No temptation has overtaken you except what is common to mankind. And God is faithful; he will not let you be tempted beyond what you can bear. But when you are tempted, he will also provide a way out so that you can endure it. Therefore, my dear friends, flee from idolatry.[81]

Life is not just a walk in the park. As humans, we must use our decision muscles daily to stay on the path that God has laid out for us. But He doesn't just abandon you to this journey. He is ahead of you, and He knows what is in your future. It encourages me that my good and grace-filled Heavenly Father knows how difficult I find life. He knows how hard it is for you to live in a world full of people denying God by their worldview and through their lifestyles. Know that in the midst of your trials, and even persecution, God is there with you.

Salvation Is Not a Business Deal

As we discussed earlier in the book, salvation is precious. One saying I have heard is that salvation is a "second chance." I get what people are saying. They want to convey the idea that we can start afresh with God, with a clean slate. While it is true that we are new creations in Christ,[82] it is much more than merely a second chance. God is not saying to us, "try me out for free," like a lawnmowing service. Nor is God saying to us, "I'll give you one last chance to behave well." No way! God is, first and foremost, a Father. When He adopts a person, He calls them His own. The Apostle Paul tells us: "We are God's handiwork, created in Christ Jesus to do good works, which God prepared in advance for us to do."[83]

God Remains Your Father

Imagine you had a daughter named Sally. One day, you catch Sally playing with matches and burning your brand-new carpet. Naturally, most parents would have a strong reaction to this reckless act. But would you "fire" Sally and tell her to find a new family? Of course not! She's your child!

Many people view God purely as a superstitious figure like Santa Claus. Santa is the kind of persona that we try to keep at arm's length with our good deeds. Not God. God is our Father. Check out the story of the Prodigal Son and his father. The father said, "this son of mine was dead and is alive again; he was lost and is found."[84] Focusing on the things you do, or don't do, for God, keeps Him at arm's length. By faith, I challenge you to stop letting your performance dictate how you feel. Instead, rejoice every day that you belong to Him. Do it whether your day is going well, or whether it's a stinker.

Do you ever act out when you don't feel "right?" Be honest with yourself and God. He knows anyway. There are times when my children will go against my wishes, and do things that I told them not to do. Then, once we are finished having the tough conversation, they often receive a hug from me. I want them to know that the relationship is stable.

Just the other day, my eldest daughter and I were walking up the stairs at home. She was eager to race up the stairs, but I grabbed her arm and reminded her, "If you run in the house, you might get hurt." After that, I let go of her arm. Off she went running—like a rocket! Then she tried to cut the corner in the hallway and smacked her forehead on the wall. She stopped and rubbed her forehead. Fighting tears, she came back to me and buried her sad face in my thigh. I am relieved she learned this lesson now, while she's little.

We adults may try to hide it, but we all need reassurance in relationships. God wants you to know that you are His. In fact, when Jesus was baptized, God spoke in an audible voice, saying He was pleased with Jesus, His Son.[85] You might think this only applies to Jesus. Guess again. The Bible tells us that Jesus was the "firstborn among many brothers and sisters."[86]

God the Father is the architect. He is the author. He can communicate through people, circumstances, and His Word—the Bible. Think of the Bible as God's fingerprint. By using the Bible (with the help of the Holy Spirit), we can evaluate what is from God and what isn't. It is this fingerprint that allows you to discover the truth about God, and the truth about yourself. There is nobody who grows up with a perfect family or perfect circumstances. As children, we picked up a range of experiences, which led to beliefs and habits. Children learn how to value themselves when people around them place value on them. It's a classic case of "monkey-see-monkey-do."

Say Goodbye to Shame

As a 14-year-old, I went to a Christian camp in the countryside. We slept in tents and didn't shower for four days. We enjoyed heaps of activities. The most intense was abseiling—which is essentially descending a cliff with a rope and harness. I am grateful for that harness! There were also mud-fights, but that's not my style. I like to be clean.

Somehow I can't forget what happened the first time I set foot in that campground. A boy walked past, looked straight at me and said, "hello," and kept walking. This may not seem like a big deal to you, but by that time I had been through close to a decade at school where kids had picked on me and avoided me. That simple greeting was unexpected and bypassed my defenses. I couldn't believe I would be accepted by my peers. It broke my pattern and made me curious. "Why did he say that? Does he want something from me?" The only time kids at school were nice to me was when they wanted something. God the Father had my attention. This was the start of my journey out of shame.

This—like many other aspects of spiritual growth—is a process that happens in stages. One day, as an adult, I was in a church service where the presence of God was evident through the praise and worship. I remember God speaking to my spirit (basically, He put the thought in my mind; there is no other way to explain it). He asked me, "Stuart, do you believe that I took your shame?" I thought for a moment, and then said, "Yes, I believe." At that moment, a surge of energy went through me, and I felt different. I felt clean.

Each time I have a profound experience like that, I become more and more whole. God wants this for you too.

Grace

God wants to be your perfect Father. He is both able and willing to infuse you with His grace so that you can shine like a star in a darkened world.[87] For you, the concept of a father may be an unpleasant one, or, perhaps, it is something you have not considered. Your earthly father may have been distant, indifferent, or abusive—if he was in your life at all.

While that reality may not change, God's invitation to you is to become His child. Even I was skeptical and brought along my preconceived idea of who God is. Time and time again, I experience something that proves my hypothesis wrong. God is chipping away at me like a marble statue, and revealing my true identity as His child.

Building Blocks

- Not only have you been made right with God, but you have also been adopted into His family.
- God remains your Father, even when you fail.
- God wants you to be whole, more than you want to be whole.

8

GOD IS WITH YOU
LISTEN TO GOD THE HOLY SPIRIT

My friend

When I was an exchange student in Tokyo, Japan, in my early twenties, I met a girl named Hanako.

At the end of a full day of classes—which were typically three to six hours a day—I stepped outside into the courtyard with a few classmates. We chatted in Japanese. By then, we were all reasonably comfortable with speaking the language, since English was not common among all the international students.

After my classmates left for the subway station, I saw a smiling Japanese girl sidling up to me, together with a friend of hers. She bowed and said to me in Japanese, "Hey, I saw you in Mr. Nakamura's history class!" We chatted briefly, exchanged phone numbers, and then parted ways.

Being a university student in a foreign land, this was a buzz. I told myself, this is an opportunity to make a new local friend and improve my linguistic skills along the way. I was kidding myself.

We met for lunch soon after, off-campus. In my usual style, I kept things casual—perhaps too casual. I can't help thinking that it was some kind of "date." I suspected this because of the way she reacted to my eating technique! One thing I did not have much of at the time was discernment—being able to work out if I needed to take an opportunity, or simply pull out. This is not a commentary on Hanako; rather I want to highlight the issues I had with personal boundaries.

A few weeks after this lunch date, I had a chance encounter with Hanako on campus. I greeted her with a smile, "Hi Hanako! Long time no see!" She kept walking as if she'd never seen me before. Ouch. Did I misunderstand her intentions? Naturally, I was confused.

However, this was not the last time I heard from her. A year later, I received a message from you-know-who:

"Hi Stuart, do you want to catch up sometime? From Hanako. ^_^"

My curiosity got the better of me. I replied, "Sure!" and promptly set a date. Meanwhile, I found myself trying to suppress the thoughts that meeting Hanako again wasn't a good idea. Deep down I knew it was not the right decision. I even started searching for Bible verses to justify my logic. Interestingly, despite the past issues we had, I still wanted to meet her again for some reason. (Hey, I won't try to hide that I was naive!) In pressing forward, I refused to listen to my friend, the Holy Spirit, but more on that later.

The day came for Hanako and I to meet again. To my surprise, I woke up feeling ill—so ill I could barely get out of bed. I texted Hanako:

"Hi Hanako, I know we were supposed to meet today, but I woke up feeling really sick! Sorry—maybe we should do this another time."

"Hi Stuart, how odd. Let's meet another day."

This time, I conceded defeat. I was smart enough to know this was not a simple coincidence. It was the last time I contacted Hanako. It wasn't her fault, but God cared enough to keep me from a relationship that would have harmed us both. Looking back, I am so grateful.

The story doesn't end there. A day or two after that experience, I woke up, looking straight at the ceiling of the room in which I was staying. The room was dark. The bluish-white street light seeped in through the blinds and spread in a fan formation across the ceiling. At this point, I could feel the presence of God in the room. The only feeling I would compare this to would be static electricity.

I had a strong desire to pray. The conversation unfolded like this:

"God, I feel like I need to pray about something, but I am not sure what."

"Pray about your life."

"My life? The only thing I really want to pray for is my future wife."

"Okay then. Pray that you will know the name of your future wife this year."

"What? Well, nothing to lose. I pray that I will know the name of my future wife this year."

I had my doubts whether anything would happen. I returned to Australia a few weeks later and packed my belongings for my move to Sydney. I had been accepted into a postgraduate course that was not available in my hometown. Mere weeks after the conversation with God in that guest room, I met the girl that I now proudly call my wife. Together we have two children and serve God as a family.

The Holy Spirit in Your Life

Why did I share this story? To demonstrate my way with women? Hardly. Back when I met my wife, I used to eat like a starving chipmunk. This story illustrates something that the Holy Spirit did in my life that is still paying dividends today. My life over the last twenty years has been enriched by a relationship with the Holy Spirit, and I hope you get to know Him too.

Who is the Holy Spirit?

You and I, as human beings, have three distinct parts—soul, body, and spirit. After all, we are made in the image of God, who has those same three parts. God too has a soul (God the Father), a body (God the Son—Jesus Christ) and a spirit (the Holy Spirit). God thinks and loves with His soul, gives with His body, and speaks by His Holy Spirit.

Having the Holy Spirit in your life will change your approach to many things. One of these is your approach to obedience. In the book of Exodus, we see the people of Israel learning about God's laws for the first time. On Mount Sinai, God wrote down His laws on two stone tablets and gave them to Moses. It was soon clear that the people were not able to keep God's law.

Think about this: you live with a spouse or housemate. He or she goes out for the day and leaves you a note telling you what groceries to buy. Let's just say you were asked to buy a bottle of milk and a carton of eggs. How do you know whether to buy low-fat milk or whole milk? Organic eggs, free range eggs, or regular eggs? You can't ask a question of someone who is not present (unless, of course, you have a cell phone). This means that you are left to your own devices (pun intended). You must rely on your own ability to discern—your own wisdom.

God does not abandon us.[88] He has not abandoned you and He never will. He is with you always.[89] He loves you so much that He gave His one and only Son for you,[90] and He came to live inside you by the Holy Spirit![91] You can ask Him any question, anytime. His wisdom is on tap 24/7. You will never be alone again. Earlier in this chapter, I told the story of me hearing from the Holy Spirit. My problem was not whether God was speaking. My problem was that I did not want to hear the truth. I am grateful for the kindness of God that leads us to change our destructive ways.[92]

The Greatest Gift

Jesus spoke to His disciples about the best gift they could ever hope to receive. He said:

> Which of you fathers, if your son asks for a fish, will give him a snake instead? Or if he asks for an egg, will give him a scorpion? If you then, though you are evil, know how to give good gifts to your children, how much more will your Father in heaven give the Holy Spirit to those who ask him![93]

Yes, the Holy Spirit is the best gift you could ever ask for. I didn't understand this for a long time. I desperately wanted material things. I wanted recognition. Now that I have been around longer and experienced some good and some hard times, I can tell you that the Holy Spirit is definitely the greatest gift—better than anything else you could possibly ask for in this world. The Holy Spirit is humble like a servant, yet He is the embodiment of all of God's power. As the Prophet Isaiah wrote:

> Whether you turn to the right or to the left, your ears will hear a voice behind you, saying, "This is the way; walk in it."[94]

I have never known any other friend like the Holy Spirit. Make sure you get to know Him too.

Things the Holy Spirit Does Not Say

Whenever we refer to the Holy Spirit speaking, it is not necessarily always a voice you can hear with your ears—although some people claim to have experienced this. Most of the time, the Holy Spirit speaks directly into your mind. Does that sound far-fetched? Hang on! You are a spiritual being, so that means that there are things going on all around you that you cannot perceive with your five senses. There is some degree of truth to the cartoon characters being counseled by tiny angels and devils on their shoulders.

The Bible says that Jesus comes to knock on the door of your heart, so He can come in and have a relationship with you.[95] Similarly, our enemy, the devil, likes to crouch at the door of your heart and wait for an opportunity to hijack your life.[96] Why else would Cain kill Abel? Surely Cain had other options when he was feeling disappointed with God. Even from the dawn of time, the enemy has been there, persuading humankind to do destructive things.[97]

At times, it may feel like the voice in your head is nagging you. Fortunately, this is not God. Remember, not every idea that comes into your head is God. Also, not every thought you have is caused by what you had for lunch. You need to test every thought and apprehend rogue thoughts before they sabotage you.[98]

If a voice is accusing you, it is not the Holy Spirit. God does not accuse. That is what the devil does.[99] Remember, as a child of God, there is no longer any accusation that the enemy can rightfully throw at you.[100] Jesus has paid the price for you, and you are legally acquitted in the courtroom of Heaven.[101] Keep this in mind when you are seeking to hear from God.

The Holy Spirit will also never contradict the Word of God. James, the brother of Jesus, tells us that God does not change like shifting shadows.[102] James would know firsthand about the nature of God. Jesus told us, "Anyone who has seen me has seen the father."[103] He is dependable, and will not move the goal posts on you.

Finally, the Holy Spirit will never threaten you with punishment or attempt to control you with fear. That is one of the enemy's many schemes to derail you.[104]

Things the Holy Spirit Says

The Holy Spirit will bring to your remembrance the things that Jesus has taught you.[105] The Holy Spirit has a knack for bringing back information out of your mental repository, just when you need it. Because of this, the more regularly you spend time reading, listening to, and studying His Word, the better you will be at discerning His voice.[106] You get out what you put in. Keep reading the Bible, praying, and listening to good teaching, even when you don't feel like you have any particular struggle. Don't view it as something you "have to do" or as a religious activity—it is incredibly important to your spiritual health. Keep God's thoughts and worldview at the forefront of your mind. Just like physical exercise, the more you study God's Word, the more you will want to do it. Through these actions, you are programming your mind for victory, which we will examine more closely in Part 4 of this book.

The Holy Spirit also enables you to experience God's love. As we covered in an earlier chapter, Romans Chapter 5 tells us that hope does not disappoint us, because the Holy Spirit pours God's love into us.[107] The Holy Spirit teaches you how to pray—meaning He helps you communicate with God. He even prays on our behalf when we have no words.[108] The Holy Spirit is your friend.

In fact, the Holy Spirit is the most encouraging person in the universe. Some of the most amazing times I have had in His presence are the times when He has encouraged me in situations I was facing. In some of the hardest times in my life, where my mind was full of dread, I have dared to ask the Holy Spirit, "What do You want to say to me right now?" Sometimes, all He says back is, "You are doing well," or "Keep going"—simple words that penetrate darkness like a flashlight. He might point me to scripture, a book, or a person. You may think there is nobody around that can encourage you, but the Holy Spirit is a black-belt encourager who will not only encourage you, He will teach you to internalize encouragement so you can encourage yourself.[109]

Like the Wind

Jesus talks about the Holy Spirit as being like the wind:

> The wind blows wherever it pleases. You hear its sound, but you cannot tell where it comes from or where it is going. So it is with everyone born of the Spirit.[110]

If you are in Christ, you are born of the Spirit—the Holy Spirit. He will lead you down a path that is not always obvious, but it is a path to true significance. Remember what Jesus says, that the road that leads to life is narrow, and the wide road leads to destruction.[111] People around you may be perplexed by the choices you make at times and may disagree with your views. Don't worry. Focus on pleasing God, and He will reward you Himself.

So there you have it. This is just a brief introduction to the Holy Spirit. Regardless of where you are in your life right now, I encourage you to lay down your defenses and let Him in. Get to know the Holy Spirit for yourself.

Building Blocks

- The real question is not whether God is speaking, but whether we are ready to listen.

- God's voice is not the only one competing for your headspace. Be vigilant about what thoughts you entertain.

- Diligently seek to hear God's voice, and He will lead you on the path to significance.

PART 3
PEOPLE
TOGETHER WE WIN

9

SHARED SUCCESS
TAKE PEOPLE WITH YOU

When I was a university student, I traveled to Japan for the first time to visit friends. I took a cheap digital camera with me and snapped lots of photos. I took photos of everything: buildings, food—even my host's toilet. (It was a novelty to me—after all, most toilets back home don't have a faucet on top!) I must have taken hundreds of photos during my one-month trip to Japan.

When I returned to Australia, I proceeded to show my family some of the highlights from my trip. I showed picture after picture of buildings and objects. Before long, my mother piped up and remarked, "Where are all the people?" It hadn't occurred to me that I had taken almost no photos of people on my trip! To someone else looking at my photo album, I hadn't met anyone.

People

That remark took me by surprise, but looking back I realize that my vision for my future had no people in it. Sure, God was in it somewhere, but I had created a fantasy vision where I was independently successful. I suppose I had gotten used to doing things solo. Ever since my school days, I spent a whole lot of time alone. Perhaps I viewed other people as an inconvenience. Perhaps they stood between me and success. I felt that people could not be trusted with what was most valuable to me. I also had plenty of experience being hurt by others and spent years of my life holding onto offense.

Trust

If you struggle to trust people, then start by trusting God. The Bible tells us that God Himself will never let us down.[112] He is not fickle like shadows are—pointing one way in the morning and another way in the afternoon.[113] He is not a human being like us so rest assured He will never lie to you.[114]

In my case, the journey of involving people in my life required me to leave my comfort zone behind. Initially, the main way I did this was by attending more and more social events after church. For a long time, I did not feel all that comfortable in those situations, but as I persevered my threshold for pain increased. I realized that not only was I capable of interacting with other people, but I also had something to offer them.

Secret Pain

I thought I was a forgiving person, but one day, God showed me my blind spot. I was too proud to admit that I was offended by a former leader in my church. Without giving too much away, I perceived that I was mistreated by this person. I carried this hurt in my soul for over a decade, and little by little my relationship with God started to suffer. It was like my spiritual "bucket" had developed a hole, and I was leaking all the time.

I started to struggle to praise God—even to the most anointed music. I began to doubt the sincerity of my leaders. Then, I started to suspect all spiritual leaders of being untrustworthy. Eventually, I even stopped reading my Bible for a time. I thought to myself, "What's the point?" Due to this issue of unforgiveness in my heart, I found myself gradually doing less volunteer ministry at church, until I stopped altogether. You may think you are above this happening to you, but be on your guard. I am truly grateful for God's kindness to me during this time. After all, His kindness leads us to repentance—to change our ways.[115]

One day in church, something unexpected happened. It was as if God put His finger on my unforgiveness and said, "Stuart, it's time to let this go. You cannot move forward into your future if you are still holding onto this." I proceeded to write a letter to the offender—not so I could send it but so that I could recall what happened and then verbalize the pain I had refused to feel.

This exercise solicited strong and painful emotions. The only way to describe it was like breathing out fire. These feelings came with a force that many Christians would view as unacceptable—even sinful. Keep in mind that the Bible does not say, "anger is a sin." Rather, it says, "in your anger do not sin."[116] Even Jesus Himself—though often caricatured to be "meek and mild"—felt angry sometimes, and He had no trouble letting people know. The key point here is what you decide to do next. Are you going to use your anger to bring positive change, or to bring division?

Once this secret pain was out in the open, I was able to use my anger for good. I turned my paper over and wrote this:

> I am making a commitment today to forgive you. In the name of Jesus, I release you from all wrongdoing, whether

intentional or unintentional. I commit to praying for your blessing and restoration . . . Now that I can look back and see the past more clearly, I can also see you were going through a difficult time too. I am no longer judge over you. I love you in the name of Jesus.

It is important to note that there is no guarantee that I will ever see this person again, or that we will ever reconcile. The good news is that you can release people, even if they are out of your life for whatever reason—and even if they never say sorry. After all, Jesus didn't wait for you to say sorry before He forgave you on the cross:

> . . . God demonstrates his own love for us in this: While we were still sinners, Christ died for us.[117]

Once I completed the letter, the suspicious thoughts I used to have about spiritual leaders ceased immediately. I am no longer afraid of submitting to leaders that God has strategically placed over me, and I am excited about what the future holds. My story is proof that prompt conflict resolution is better for everyone involved—regardless of how big or small the problem is. The earlier you process the pain of being hurt, the better.

Before we move on, I do not want to make light of anything that may have happened to you in your own life. I may not have been through the same things as you, but I know what it is like to hurt. On that note, please take heed when Jesus says: ". . . if you refuse to forgive others, your Father will not forgive your sins."[118] Let's face it: forgiveness is a process, and working through the feelings may be a decision you need to make every single day. But whatever you do, make sure you decide to forgive, so that you can live as a forgiven child of God, in this life and for eternity.

For a more comprehensive discussion on the topic of forgiveness, I highly recommend the book *The Bait of Satan*, by John Bevere. This book was a part of my own breakthrough, and I believe it will help connect you with the truth about offense and forgiveness.

Understanding the power of forgiveness is also indispensable when trying to connect better with people. You were not designed to live alone but in partnership with God and people. God said of Adam, the first man in recorded history, "It is not good for man to be alone."[119] The Apostle Paul stresses to us the importance of "not giving up meeting together, as some are in the habit of doing, but encouraging one another—and all the more as you see the Day approaching."[120]

We're Better Together

We see that Nehemiah started his building project alone, but he was not alone for long. Not only did he have people with him, but he also enlisted local help to tackle the enormous task of rebuilding the wall of Jerusalem. Nehemiah tells his story like this:

> I went to Jerusalem, and after staying there three days I set out during the night with a few others. I had not told anyone what my God had put in my heart to do for Jerusalem. There were no mounts with me except the one I was riding on. By night I went out through the Valley Gate toward the Jackal Well and the Dung Gate, examining the walls of Jerusalem, which had been broken down, and its gates, which had been destroyed by fire. Then I moved on toward the Fountain Gate and the King's Pool, but there was not enough room for my mount to get through; so I went up the valley by night, examining the wall. Finally, I turned back and reentered through the Valley Gate. The officials did not

know where I had gone or what I was doing, because as yet I had said nothing to the Jews or the priests or nobles or officials or any others who would be doing the work. Then I said to them, "You see the trouble we are in: Jerusalem lies in ruins, and its gates have been burned with fire. Come, let us rebuild the wall of Jerusalem, and we will no longer be in disgrace." I also told them about the gracious hand of my God on me and what the king had said to me. They replied, "Let us start rebuilding." So they began this good work. But when Sanballat the Horonite, Tobiah the Ammonite official and Geshem the Arab heard about it, they mocked and ridiculed us. "What is this you are doing?" they asked. "Are you rebelling against the king?"[121]

Nehemiah did a few important things here. First, he waited for the right people to be on his team. In your life, do not let just anybody who comes along help you build your spiritual maturity. While all people have value in the eyes of God, not all people are worthy of your trust when it comes to your inner life. Follow Jesus' example when people are drawn to you: "Jesus did not entrust Himself to them, for He knew all men."[122] It is worth waiting longer to connect deeply with the right people. Connecting too deeply with the wrong people can cause pain which is mostly preventable. Ask God to send you people whom you can trust with your inner life.

Secondly, Nehemiah shared his vision, which was about a wall. In Chapter 2, we examined how important it is to know where you are, and where you want to go. Now that you have a clear vision, and the right people to tell, invite these trusted people to be part of your vision. Do not let yourself be bound by a "burden mentality" where needing other people makes you weak. That is such a lie. Instead, practice politely, yet boldly, asking for help. For example, you may need someone to keep you accountable for staying connected to God. You may need someone to pray with you on a regular basis. You may simply need someone to listen. Again, do not give away all your "cards" straight away. Give these people a little piece of responsibility at a time, so that they can prove themselves trustworthy.

Finally, make use of your newfound network when accusation comes. In the above passage, Sanballat, Tobiah, and Geshem came against Nehemiah, asking, "Are you rebelling against the king?"[123] Hang on a second! Were they rebelling against the king? Hardly! Remember that not long before this event, the king gave Nehemiah letters of authority and provision to rebuild the wall. The king even sent soldiers to guard Nehemiah on his journey.[124] Knowing all this, Nehemiah responded to this accusation, with bold defiance, saying, "The God of heaven will give us success."[125] Notice that *us* is plural. This was not "The Nehemiah Show." Nehemiah not only had God's authority and provision, but a group of supportive people. Friend, I pray that you too would develop a group of people like this in your life. Have faith that God will bring people around you who accept you, but love you too much to let you wallow in mediocrity. These people help you gain the boldness to say, "The God of heaven will give us success."

When people resist you or don't understand

This sounds wonderful to have people around you supporting you and helping you grow stronger in God. We naturally expect that if God allowed someone to be in our lives, then this person will be positive to us at all times. This is not always the case. Some people in your life may appear to be working against you. This may seem counterintuitive to you. It was for me. Then God showed me what I am about to share with you. Let's examine the story of Moses and Pharaoh.

Moses was chosen to deliver the people of Israel from captivity in Egypt. On multiple occasions, Moses approached

Pharaoh and petitioned him to let the people of Israel go free. God revealed His plan to Moses in this way:

> Now when the LORD spoke to Moses in Egypt, he said to him, "I am the LORD. Tell Pharaoh king of Egypt everything I tell you." But Moses said to the LORD, "Since I speak with faltering lips, why would Pharaoh listen to me?" Then the LORD said to Moses, "See, I have made you like God to Pharaoh, and your brother Aaron will be your prophet. You are to say everything I command you, and your brother Aaron is to tell Pharaoh to let the Israelites go out of his country. But I will harden Pharaoh's heart, and though I multiply my signs and wonders in Egypt, he will not listen to you. Then I will lay my hand on Egypt and with mighty acts of judgment I will bring out my divisions, my people the Israelites. And the Egyptians will know that I am the LORD when I stretch out my hand against Egypt and bring the Israelites out of it."[126]

I have a question for you. Who did God say would harden Pharaoh's heart? Perhaps you need to read that passage again. Was it Moses? Was it Pharaoh's advisers or magicians? No. It was God Himself. Huh? What was God's motivation for doing this? Wouldn't God want to make this whole deliverance thing easier for Moses? It seems almost sadistic. Yet, God had an amazing plan. Part of this plan was to show the Egyptians just how powerful He is. The other part of God's plan here, I believe, was to test Moses' resolve to follow through with his mission. In the above passage, Moses even remarked to God that he had faltering lips. He lacked self-confidence.

There may be people in your life like Pharaoh. These people may even be in your own family. These people may not even be able to see the obvious good in your life. They may be overly critical of you. Perhaps you are following Jesus, and they are not. Or maybe they are too. No matter what you do or say, they may still oppose you or disagree with you. This may feel incredibly discouraging, but don't worry. God can use this resistance to make you stronger. Even right now, He is preparing you for your calling. He did it for Moses, and He will do it for you too. Don't give up when there is resistance. Instead, lean on God more. Do what David did when his allies threatened to stone him. The Bible says, "David encouraged himself in the Lord his God."[127]

Here, David did something very wise. He refused to bear his distress on his own, and, instead, he went to God in prayer and worship. Never forget what God can do for you. He can do far more in your life then you could ever do for yourself. He can bring you through trials, regardless of whether you have the support of other people or not. He is waiting for you to look to Him. Notice again how David understood abandonment, yet maintained confidence in God:

> Though my mother and father forsake me, the Lord will receive me.[128]

Yes, people are an important part of your journey towards spiritual maturity—building the wall of protection around your life. But, whenever you cannot get the input you need from people, it is a sign that you need to take a step back and look to God.

Implications

I want to encourage you. Don't give up on people altogether. Don't throw the baby out with the bathwater! People are an integral part of God's plan for you. If you are suffering as a result of previous relationships, do not hesitate to bring God in. Ask Him to send you people you can trust, and who can trust you. In some cases, it may be appropriate to visit a qualified counselor to help you work through these things. There is no shame in that. Regardless, don't let yourself drift into permanent isolation. You were made for connection.

Doing life with others is not always easy. There are differences of opinion, old habits, and the fact that other people have different battle scars to us. Those differing life and educational experiences can cause all kinds of misunderstandings. Yet this diversity is part of what makes life interesting.

Could you imagine what it would be like to be Nehemiah, growing up in a culture other than his own, and leaving that place to find his own people? That is a huge upheaval, and he would have had to deal with the differences in his new environment. He went from the king's palace to a ruined city wall. He went from a place of comfort and perceived importance, to a place of discomfort and true significance.

Trusting others can be a challenge also, especially if they have let you down in the past. This may sound cliché, but ensure you do unto others what you want them to do for you.[129] Set expectations of how you want to be treated, by modeling the behavior you want to see.

Remember Paul's words: "for God gave us a spirit not of fear but of power and love and self-control."[130] I hear people use the term self-control when they are trying to eat right, stick to a budget, or adhere to an exercise program. I also like to think about it this way: you cannot control anyone else. You can only control yourself. Right there, this opens up so many possibilities.

You can change, even if everyone else stays the same.

Building Blocks

- People are a key part of God's plan for your future.

- Learning how to release offense and forgive will keep you in the game.

- God can work through people who resist you, just as much as people who accommodate you.

10

LET GOD PICK
CONNECT WITH THE RIGHT PEOPLE

"Argh, it's that guy with the camera again."

Once upon a time, I encountered a guy at church. His face is still imprinted in my memory. Let's call him Frank. Now, Frank was usually smiling, but I suspected he was just going through the motions. He came across as a guy on the edge of the social group at church. Perhaps he did not know how to break the ice.

Every time I saw Frank, he had a professional-looking camera hanging around his neck. Before the Sunday service started, he would walk around the room, looking to engage someone in conversation. He would say things like, "Hey check out the photos I took with my camera." I have nothing against cameras, but it seemed that his camera was the only way he could start a conversation. That is a problem.

One Sunday, Frank showed me his camera. I had a quick look at his photos, but then I felt compelled to confront him.

I told him, "Frank, you don't need that camera to start a conversation. People here don't need gimmicks to be interested in others. They want to know the real you. How about you leave your camera at home next Sunday? Be yourself. Be confident that people will appreciate you—for you."

Frank paused for a moment, nodded thoughtfully and thanked me. As I write these words, I have not seen Frank in over a decade, but I have faith that our brief conversation helped him to challenge detrimental beliefs about himself.

Do you struggle to be yourself around people? If you're like me, at times, it can be the hardest to feel accepted in a local church—amongst the people that should be the most accepting. Why? Most people are mutually afraid of vulnerability—of being exposed. Usually, person A is waiting for person B to open up, and person B is waiting for person A to do the same. This creates a chicken-or-the-egg dilemma. Look at it as our general reluctance to share. I am not talking about what you do for fun, or your favorite restaurant. I am talking about your beliefs, thoughts, dreams, and aspirations. There is a time and a place to share the shallow things, but everybody needs somebody to confide in.

If you're anything like me, you probably try to pick carefully who you hang out with. After all, you want to be around people who make you feel safe. If you're like me, you have probably also tried to befriend people to improve your popularity. Let me suggest something much better than both of those methods: let God pick.

How does that work? Does this mean we just sit under a tree and wait for relationships to "happen" to us? Not at all. Instead, we invest time networking with people. We try to remember people's names. We look for small ways to serve those around us. We make an effort with small talk. We seek out small groups in the church where we can grow. Then, out of your obedience, God can provide people who can support you.

When Nehemiah set out to build the wall of Jerusalem, he started with no one around him. What makes me think that? Simple, nobody else is mentioned by name at the beginning of the story. We are told in the story that, when Nehemiah asked the king of Babylon for help, God provided richly for Nehemiah. The king lent his authority to Nehemiah. The king wrote letters to the governor of every district that Nehemiah was to pass through on his journey (God's authority). The king also wrote a letter to Asaph, the keeper of the king's forest, to request supplies (God's provision). And finally, the king sent people to go with Nehemiah on the journey (God's influence).

These people are the focus of this chapter.

I believe that—quite often—the people that God picks for you are not those you would naturally choose. On the outside, they may look different and have different interests. I can tell you from experience though that God knows best. For this reason, be polite and say hello to whoever is around you. You never know when a connection might form.

When you are open to developing connections with others and trust God to bring the right people, you will be rewarded. What kind of people does God bring? Let's look at the main traits they possess, by looking at the acronym PICK. Let's explore the acronym:

- **P**leasant
- **I**ntersection
- **C**hrist-centered
- **K**ind

Pleasant

Proverbs 27:9 says, "Perfume and incense bring joy to the heart, and the pleasantness of a friend springs from their heartfelt advice."[131] The Bible talks a lot about aromas. One of the most common mentions of *aroma* is in the first five books of the Bible, where God's people gave Him offerings—especially burnt offerings—which sent up a pleasing aroma before Him.

If you are in Christ, you are "to God the pleasing aroma of Christ among those who are being saved and those who are perishing. To the one we are an aroma that brings death; to the other, an aroma that brings life . . ."[132]

The way someone smells is important. I have a good friend from high-school. He loved sports, but back then he did not shower every day. Being outside with him was fine, but indoors? Let's just say it was hard!

But I am not talking about the way someone smells physically. I am talking about how they smell "spiritually." The aromas that please people are not necessarily the same aromas that please God. Having someone close to you who always tells you what you want to hear will end up keeping you stuck in life. You need people in your life who can tell you the truth when you most need to hear it.

Before these people are loyal to you, they are loyal to Jesus and His interests in your life. They can be truth tellers when they need to be. They would much rather tell you the truth that helps you to grow as a person, than to abdicate their responsibility by giving you endless compliments. In the book of Proverbs, we are told that "wounds from a friend can be trusted, but an enemy multiplies kisses."[133]

Intersection

The Apostle Paul talks about the concept of the Body of Christ. Simply put, every person who follows Christ has a unique skill set, gifting, and purpose. Just like a human body, the foot cannot say, "because I am not an eye, I do not belong to the body."[134] Every person in the body of Christ is needed because of what they have to offer.

I believe this concept goes even further. Other people benefit from your unique skill set, gifting, and purpose. They also benefit from your unique personality, background, and life experience. Several times in my life, I can remember meeting people who had a long-term impact on my life. They did not necessarily do anything unusual. In fact, they impacted me just by being themselves.

An example of this was when I moved to a different middle school and made a new friend. This friend—I'll call him James—simply involved me in his life. Occasionally, he would just call me to catch up. No one had ever done that before. In the beginning, I was surprised by his behavior and didn't know to say. But that experience built my confidence. James and I have since parted ways, started our careers, and started our families, but I am still blessed to see him from time to time.

Another person in my life who has rubbed off on me in a special way is my wife, Cherie. One of the things that Cherie taught me early on was how to be generous. As the years go by, I am getting better at being generous. When I lived in Japan, Cherie tells me that because I never fought over the bill, most of my friends would save face and just pay the bill. Maybe it's true. I just figured I had really nice friends.

I should add that God can also use other people through their negative traits as well as their positive traits. Maybe there are people in your life who talk too much, are always late, or irritate you by their sheer lack of tact. For instance, I love talking, and perhaps a little bit too much, so my good Father God saw fit to surround me with people that either talk too much, don't listen, constantly interrupt me, or all of the above. I must say, I am getting better at listening to others as a result.

In short, God is adept at bringing people into your life that you can help, and who can help you. These people may not have been your first choice or second choice, but they have what you need.

Christ-Centered

This point may come across as obvious, but there are particular aspects of Christ-centered relationships that are unique and exclusive. It is these very attributes that show the world we are His disciples.

First, we love one another. Jesus once said to His disciples, "A new command I give you: Love one another. As I have loved you, so you must love one another. By this everyone will know that you are my disciples, if you love one another."[135] What does it mean to love one another? In the world we live in, so many people profess to know what love is and isn't. But the way Jesus defines love seems foreign to them. Jesus said, "Greater love has no one than this: to lay down one's life for one's friends."[136] There is a sacrificial aspect to this love. There is a sense that people with a Christ-centered relationship are willing to go out of their way to help each other. I believe that it is impossible to be a fairweather friend in a Christ-centered relationship. The focus is never getting something. Rather, the focus is pleasing Jesus by serving the person in front of you.

Next, people in Christ-centred relationships no longer see themselves from a worldly point of view.[137] They see each other as new creations in Christ. The Apostle Paul tells us that, "If anyone is in Christ, a new creation has come: The old has gone, the new is here!"[138] Whether you are connected to a friend, or if you are married to a person, it is essential that you view them as being hand-picked by God to be in your life. This does not mean that they are perfect, or that they will not offend you at times. In fact, it is fair to say that God will often put people in your life who will sharpen you—using their positive traits *and* their negative traits. The book of Proverbs tells us, "As iron sharpens iron, so one person sharpens another."[139]

Do my friends have to be believers?

At this juncture, it is worth noting that God can use unbelievers to help you grow and support you as a person. In fact, you may be the best testimony of Christ that they ever see. In some cases, you might lose contact with friends or even family when you follow Christ, but Jesus Himself said, "Whoever is not against you is for you."[140] Because every situation is different, involve God in any decision that you make regarding your friendships. The bottom line is, if you are determined to follow Christ, then the people who are allowed to speak wisdom into your life need to have the aroma of Christ. It is not to say that other people cannot be involved in your life, but make sure the most influential voices in your ears are those submitted to Christ.

Kindness

We are told in the book of Romans that, "God's kindness is intended to lead you to repentance."[141] We all need people who can help us change—not just behaviors, but mindsets and beliefs. People cannot be coerced or forced into changing their minds. They need to be convinced that it is the right thing. The existence of condemnation in the world makes it all the harder for us to change. But get this: God loves us so much that He sent His Son to die for us *first*—before we did anything to change.[142] This is great news.

Kind people also practice what I call *positive accountability*. Many years ago when I attended the youth ministry at my church, it was very common to hear about accountability partners. The main focus of these groups, as I perceived, was to help young people steer clear of certain taboo sins such as sexual sin. Accountability is important, and I am clearly not against it, but for me individually, it meant that I focused heavily on what I should *not* be doing. If you are trying to improve your thought life, for example, focusing on what you don't want to think about will just make it worse. Let's try a famous experiment: "Whatever you do, do not think about elephants." If you're like me, when you read those words, you immediately think about elephants—with their long snake-like trunks and circular feet. Instead, find something you can replace those thoughts with. Try something positive like physical exercise, playing a musical instrument, spending time studying the Bible, or simply catching up with a good friend. There are so many options. Your freedom in Christ is expansive; make use of it!

In the Gospels, Jesus talks about the dangers of failing to replace a bad thing with something good. Sure, the man Jesus describes had a demon driven out, but there was no genuine life change. So what happened? The original demon took seven more demons with it, and they all went into the man.[143] If anything, the man's life got worse. So be sure to mix with people who help you replace your unhelpful patterns, rather than reinforce them.

What next?

If you're anything like me, reading about the people God wants to PICK for you will hopefully inspire you to trust God for the right people. However, while you are waiting for these people, I have a challenge for you: Be that person.

When you consciously choose to be the kind of person God can PICK, you position yourself for relationship. Whether you are seeking a friend, business partner or a marriage partner, be the best *you* that you can be, and let God do the rest. Let God PICK.

Building Blocks

- God designed us for closeness and not just for talking about the weather.

- Be friendly and trust God to bring the right people across your path.

- While you are waiting for the right people, start by being the right person.

11

FOR DIFFERENT SEASONS AND DIFFERENT REASONS
LOOK TO GOD AS YOUR SOURCE

What Now?

We know that we are better together. We also know that we get the best results when we let God PICK our social connections. Just when you start getting comfortable though, your social connections move on. This may trigger all kinds of emotions: disappointment, disillusionment, and even cynicism. What if I told you that many social connections in your life are temporary, and by design?

Let's rewind to my story in Chapter 1 about Jenny. As mentioned, Jenny stepped into my world at just the right time, and made a massive difference, just by being herself. She was a great source of encouragement for me over the next few months following the camp. Then, I lost contact with her. All of a sudden, this person that I had started relying on so much was out of the picture. It was like I was in freefall. For a time, I wondered what I was going to do next—how I was going to survive. Little did I know, that I was about to receive an invitation to church—the local church I still attend as I write this. In this new environment, it was like the floodgates opened in my life, and I started meeting an amazing group of guys. Some of these guys are still in my life today.

When Nehemiah was building the wall, he had a team of diverse people, helping him to build the wall. Different people built different parts of the wall and contributed unique value. In the same way, God brings different people at different times to build you. King Solomon tells us that there is a time for "every matter under heaven."[144] Let's face it: most things in your life are temporary. Your age is temporary. Your job is temporary. Your residential address is temporary. Your phone company is temporary. Your bank balance is temporary. (Although I hope you have more money coming in than going out!) The old adage is true: the only constant is *change*.

Dealing with Change

First of all, why do we need to say goodbye to people? In some cases, people don't even say goodbye but just drift away. Sometimes people move cities, start families, or even abandon their faith in Christ. The Apostle Paul instructs us, "if it is possible, as far as it depends on you, live at peace with everyone."[145] Paul points to the fact that you cannot control the actions of others; you can only control your own actions.

Whatever you do, don't antagonize people for leaving your life. Instead, deal with your own feelings of loss, and also any fear of abandonment you may have. You may also have given way to cynicism because some good friends have moved away. They may have been people that you depended on.

Think of it this way. There are many people that live in the same city as me that I never contact. This is pretty normal. I am not necessarily at odds with these people; we are just now in a different season of life. God handpicks people to work on specific sections of your character—your wall. Each person in your life brings a unique influence. You may be either inspired or offended by that person. In the end, if you choose to see God's hand in your life in every season you will end up blessed, and God will get the glory.

I recall hearing a story some time ago, from a friend. Let's call her Monica. Monica had a dear friend that she hadn't contacted for a long time. Monica felt guilty about neglecting this friendship. One day, she decided to call her friend to make amends. This friend's reaction surprised Monica. The friend asked, "Why are you calling me? Is there a problem?" This friend did not perceive any distance between them. Just because you don't have regular contact with someone, doesn't mean that they are gone forever. Sure, technology can help you to stay in touch. But if their circumstances change, it means that your relationship may need to change too.

When the relational landscape of your life is changing all around you, set your focus on Jesus. He is "the same yesterday and today and forever."[146] We also know, "God is not human, that he should lie . . ."[147] He is consistent, and He is consistently good. If you trust in Jesus, you have passed from death to life.[148] You have become a child of Almighty God. God, your perfect Father, will never abandon you.[149]

Facing Loneliness

To find out just how dependable God is, you need to take Him at His Word. When I was in Japan, I experienced what was an unusual Christmas Day. In my home country of Australia, this is the most popular holiday of the year to visit family. Instead, I was alone on a cold, overcast, and rainy December day. I saw no one the entire day. Even on this dark day in my life, God was still with me. I'm not going to pretend I was happy about being completely alone. I fought depressive thoughts that day. Sometimes I wonder how I survived on days like that. Looking back, one of my go-to moves was putting on worship music in my college dorm room and spending hours in His presence. After all, what other options did I have?

I touched on my school experience earlier on. For about five years, I had virtually no friends. In fact, when I started a new school in the seventh grade, I was asked semi-regularly by other students, "Where are your friends?" I know something about the pain of isolation. It doesn't matter whether you've isolated yourself, or others have pushed you away: it still hurts.

Just remember, when you feel all alone, God Himself can become your greatest strength. Asaph the Psalmist wrote: "My flesh and my heart may fail, but God is the strength of my heart and my portion forever."[150] Moses learned to talk to God like a friend.[151] Why not you? Tell Him what's really going on inside. Finally, as Paul impressed on the church at Ephesus, "It's in Christ that we find out who we are and what we are living for."[152] While you wait for God's provision, get into His presence and stay strong.

Goodbyes

This year, my wife Cherie and I lost a dear friend to a terminal illness. We knew her for about three years, which may seem like a relatively short friendship. If you knew just how much of an impact she had on us, you would understand why this was a tough goodbye. While we grieved our loss, we rejoiced and thanked God for the long-term deposit she left in our lives. I am reminded of what Jesus said to His disciples, that fateful night when He said goodbye:

> "Very truly I tell you, unless a kernel of wheat falls to the ground and dies, it remains only a single seed. But if it dies, it produces many seeds."[153]

As a result of this friendship, my wife Cherie experienced profound healing and is now paying it forward into other women's lives. I am not implying that I have God figured out. This event had me floored. But I sure am glad that He is on the throne and not me.

Eternal Perspective

One of the most precious stories in the Bible for me personally is where the Apostle Paul said goodbye to his church friends:

> "When Paul had finished speaking, he knelt down with all of them and prayed. They all wept as they embraced him and kissed him. What grieved them the most was his statement that they would never see his face again. Then they accompanied him to the ship."[154]

It is in this story that we see Paul, not just as a rock star apostle who ministers in the Word and in the miraculous. At this moment, he is just a friend.

Have you lost a friend or other loved one? It doesn't matter what the circumstances were—it still hurts on some level. Have you processed this loss? If not, I challenge you to bring God into the situation. Let Him grieve with you. It is okay to feel sad when you lose someone—whatever the reason. The list of possible reasons is long. Maybe they simply moved away. Or maybe—like in my story earlier in the chapter—they are no longer on the earth. Just understand that God has a new chapter in store for you. In fact, before you were even born, God wrote your life in a book,[155] and that book has a wonderful ending.

Don't despair.

Building Blocks

- Many social connections in your life are temporary, by design.

- The way you respond when people exit your life will impact your future.

- There is no way around grief and loss; it must be dealt with if you are going to bounce back.

12

DON'T BE A STRANGER
BE A FRIEND

You Had Me at "Hello"

I have a long history of feeling out of place in social settings. I felt this the most at school, but there were times when I felt the same at church. At one point, there was about a six-month period where I did not go to the young adults' meetings every Saturday night. It felt like too much work. I reasoned that I did not have anything in common with the other attendees.

The following year, on the night that the young adults' ministry kicked off again at church, something happened. There was a small voice inside. I just knew I needed to go to church that Saturday night. The voice was so compelling that I felt okay about laying aside my past experience. I stepped out of my comfort zone and obeyed God.

Soon after I arrived, I noticed a guy standing by himself. I introduced myself to him, "Hi, I'm Stuart." I persisted with my friendly interrogation. It turns out he had never been to our church before—and one day he just felt an inner nudge to come visit. Not long after that, a network formed around him in the young adults ministry and they stayed on his case every week. Before long, he gave his life to Christ and started serving in the church. At the time of this writing—which is many years later—he still walks with God. It is an honor to be part of his story.

Never underestimate the power of being friendly.

I don't know about you, but most personality tests will tell you that I am an introvert. For most of my life, I have found it more convenient to go it alone and leave the mingling to the extroverts. What I didn't realize is that God made you and I with amazing personalities and that we all can add immense value to each other. While it is not possible to change our God-given temperament, it is possible to defy these limiting stereotypes of introvert and extrovert.

In fact, I spent most of my late teens intentionally leaving my comfort zone, and spending time with people wherever possible. This meant going to all kinds of house parties and staying out later than I felt comfortable. I liked going to bed early. I had my driver's license by then, so I was frequently home late on weekends (though the parties were very tame).

Meeting New People With Confidence

I was still self-conscious by the time I reached the end of high school. If it were not for God coming alongside me and coaching me through the Word of God and through people, I could not be where I am today. It is my great privilege to share some of these insights with you.

After I met my beautiful wife, I found myself living in South Korea. I was newly married, so I obviously had some companionship in my wife. On the flipside though, I was in a foreign land, could speak only broken Korean, and had very few friends around me. I was alone and vulnerable. But God was with me.

It was not uncommon for me to spend time alone in our one-room apartment. One night, I gazed out the window—the Korean skyline punctuated by red neon crosses—just knowing I needed a breakthrough in myself. I needed to be stronger. I did not just want to make it through another day: I wanted to overcome.

I believe the Holy Spirit can help us understand the Bible in many ways. One of these ways is that He can show us ideas in Scripture that are connected. That night, I had one of these moments.

There is an interesting passage in one of Paul's letters to the early church:

> But because of his great love for us, God, who is rich in mercy, made us alive with Christ even when we were dead in transgressions—it is by grace you have been saved. And God raised us up with Christ and seated us with him in the heavenly realms in Christ Jesus, in order that in the coming ages he might show the incomparable riches of his grace, expressed in his kindness to us in Christ Jesus.[156]

The main idea here is that God seated us with Christ in the heavenly realms. I always wondered what this meant. But then I saw this connection in the words of Jesus Himself—the One we are seated next to:

> Do not be afraid of those who kill the body but cannot kill the soul. Rather, be afraid of the One who can destroy both soul and body in hell.[157]

Jesus is saying something important here, that people on earth can only kill your body. That is good to know when people are against you. But, what about this part about being afraid of God? For years, I cringed when I read this verse.

But what happens when you put the two passages together?

If you belong to Christ, God has seated you next to Christ, and there is no safer place in the universe.

You may receive judgment and scorn from people, but if you are in Christ, right next to Him, you can join the Apostle Paul in saying, "... I know whom I have believed, and am convinced that he is able to guard what I have entrusted to him ..."[158] Let the throne room be your very source of security.

Take a Cue From Jesus

You may have heard it said that we should learn from Jesus and follow His example. I don't know about you, but it has not always been easy for me to extract principles from the life of Jesus—especially for the more specific questions I have. When I saw what I'm about to show you, it blew my mind. This is a scene from the book of Matthew. The Jews were asking Jesus whether they should pay taxes to the Roman government:

> Then the Pharisees went and plotted how to entangle [Jesus] in his words. And they sent their disciples to him, along with the Herodians, saying, "Teacher, we know that you are true and teach the way of God truthfully, and you do not care about anyone's opinion, for *you are not swayed by appearances* ..."[159]

The *English Standard Version* includes a footnote about the phrase "for you are not swayed by appearances." This same phrase can also mean: "*... for you do not look at people's faces.*"[160]

For me, this is a powerful image from the Greek language. In a sense, we are influenced—and in some ways even controlled—by the "faces" we habitually look at. To further illustrate this point, let's think about a small child under the age of two. These little ones are busy exploring the world, but they always do something very interesting: whenever they do something new, or fall over and hurt themselves, they look to the face of an adult. As a parent, it is important to show on your face that "everything is okay"—even if it isn't! If a small child falls over, they look to their adult to receive an interpretation of what just happened to them. It is as if to say, "Should I cry? Or am I okay?"

Remember that adults are just big children, and are subject to the same basic influences on a different scale. You have a choice to make. Will you let other people interpret your reality, or let God interpret it? Will you let other people tell you how you should feel? Or let God tell you? You are not an island. You are going to be influenced, one way or the other. These days, when something unexpected (or negative) happens, I often find myself asking the Holy Spirit, "Please interpret this event for me. What does this mean?"

Stop seeking the "face" of other people, and use all your energy to seek the "face" of God—His Presence, His answers, His help. This is not a license to be unkind to people in your life or to be selfish. Rather, when it comes to matters of your identity, and your direction in life, only God's face—His opinion—truly matters.

This, I believe, is how Jesus modeled a healthy posture in his relationships with others. God was the center of His affections and His worldview. Can you imagine how Jesus would have gone with His disciples if He did not rely completely on His Father? Simon Peter, one of Jesus' best friends, tried to tell Jesus not to go to the cross![161] The Apostle Paul famously said, "Am I now trying to win the approval of human beings, or of God? Or am I trying to please people? If I were still trying to please people, I would not be a servant of Christ."[162]

I am not saying that you should never listen to others, or that you should disregard their feelings. What I am saying is that when you listen to God, there will be specific times when you will need to say "no" to people. We often hear this concept referred to as, "having boundaries." It is the idea that you are an individual, with your own thoughts, your own ability to make decisions, and your own body. You are responsible for you. If you do not take responsibility for you, but start taking responsibility for others, you can easily fall into deception. If you give out all your resources to others—whether it be time, resources, emotions or even money—but you are not addressing your own needs, you won't be around tomorrow to serve. God cares about you, too. He values balance and does not take us from extreme to extreme. Otherwise, one moment you will find yourself serving everyone, and the next moment you will be utterly depleted and serving no one.

I am also not seeking to diminish God's ability to care for you and refresh you as you serve others. He can and does. Just be proactive in meeting your own needs—not because you are "selfish," but because you want to help even more people. Some of these things are obvious. Find out how much sleep you need per night, and carve out time for it. Find out what food nourishes you the best, and eat that food as often as possible. Find out how long you need per week to spend time with God to stay fresh—this is different for everyone. Carve out that time. Do it, because you value yourself, but even more so, because you want to honor God and the amazing future He has planned for you.

A Final Word About People

As our discussion of people draws to a close, be encouraged by a story where Jesus makes a new connection:

> The next day Jesus decided to leave for Galilee. Finding Philip, he said to him, "Follow me." Philip, like Andrew

and Peter, was from the town of Bethsaida. Philip found Nathaniel and told him, "We have found the one of whom prophets also wrote—Jesus of Nazareth." "Nazareth! Can anything good come from there?" Nathaniel asked. "Come and see" said Philip. When Jesus saw Nathaniel approaching, he said of him, "Here truly is an Israelite in whom there is no deceit." "How do you know me?" Nathaniel asked. Jesus answered, "I saw you while you were still under the fig tree before Philip called you."[163]

Nathaniel even had doubts that meeting this guy called Jesus would be worth his time. After all, Jesus came from Nazareth, which was not a trendy place back then. (Jesus was there before it was cool.) Then, once Jesus started speaking, Nathaniel was amazed at God's great power and wisdom. Let this inspire you to be diligent in your social life and wait for the right connections.

Building Blocks

- Never underestimate the power of being friendly.
- The number one key to successful relationships is to know your position in Christ.
- Let God tell you how to think, feel, and act—not people.

PART 4
PROGRAMMING
THINKING TO WIN

13

CHASING FANTASY
EMBRACE REALITY WITH GOD

I wanted the straight path . . .

When I first entered university, I had this grand vision to pursue my love of language learning. For some reason, I thought my essay writing days were over. Now that was naïve. Before I knew it, I was running around the campus at 4:45 p.m. on the due date, looking for a printer that worked.

Yes, this was not as glamorous as I had hoped, but the embarrassment didn't end there. Straight after graduating, I moved to another state to study how to be an interpreter. My eyes were soon opened to the reality of the profession. It was quite different from what I had imagined.

Do you notice a recurring theme of me doing things at the last minute? I withdrew from my interpreting course at 5:00 p.m. on the last day they processed refunds. From that point, I was in free-fall. I was living away from home, with no course, and no job. I had the belief that I could walk into a job with a reputable company as soon as I graduated. After all, my university had a high ranking. It was a rude shock when the rejection notes started pouring in. Even worse were the times where no response came. It turns out I had spent four years training for a job that only existed between my ears. What wake-up call!

Disillusioned, I found myself staying in a dormitory at a seminary—of all places. They were close to my university and had extra space. I encountered a student there in his fifties. He looked like a biker, but he was a Registered Nurse. I didn't see that coming. He was as wise as his beard was long. He could probably see the disappointment on my face. He took me aside and told me something I cannot forget: "The journey of life does not necessarily occur on a straight path. Rather, the path meanders from side to side. Open your eyes to the periphery. Keep a look out for unexpected possibilities."

That advice was timely. Mere months after that conversation, I found myself packing up all my belongings and boarding a flight to South Korea. A new chapter awaited. My fantasy plan was out the window. I was now heading for uncharted territory. Do I regret this? Not for a second! My time in South Korea was life-defining and paved the way for you to read this book.

As with the Israelites, God had a plan for me. It was through my failed postgraduate course that I met the love of my life, became a father to two beautiful children, and took some positive, though unexpected, steps forward in my career. God gave me a better future than I could have dreamt up for myself. God's mode of operation and His way of thinking couldn't be more different from ours.[164]

Often things in life will not go the way you planned, and you need to guard your heart against disappointment. But, through the bad, God can turn things around to be better in the end. It's your job to trust in Him.[165]

In this chapter, we will discuss deceptive thoughts that can derail you from your devotion to Jesus. Take a moment now before we dive in, to ask the Holy Spirit to help you deal with these confrontational concepts.

Okay, buckle your seat belt! Here we go.

Sense of Entitlement

As I learned the hard way when I graduated from university, the world did not owe me anything. I had to drop the sentence from my repertoire, "I should be able to do this." The belief that says the world owes us—or that other people owe us—is known as a sense of entitlement. This is deadly to have in your mindset because it lures you into passivity, indecision, and inaction.

In order to deal with the sense of entitlement, you need to get back to basics. King David records a profound and humbling thought in the Psalms:

> When I consider your heavens, the work of your fingers, the moon, and the stars, which you have set in place, what is mankind that you are mindful of them, human beings that you care for them?[166]

Let's get one thing straight: all of us were born sinners.[167] Being good, is not good enough. Going to a building every Sunday with a cross on it is not good enough. I am asking if you have been raised to life with Christ. Even though I am sure you were a cute baby, the reality is that you were spiritually dead from birth.[168] The Apostle Paul talks about how salvation in Jesus is a gift that we could never hope to earn:

> ... it is by grace you have been saved, through faith— and this is not from yourselves, it is the gift of God— not by works, so that no one can boast. For we are God's

handiwork, created in Christ Jesus to do good works, which God prepared in advance for us to do.[169]

If someone hands you a gift and then asks you to pay for it, it is not a gift. The gift giver chooses to give the gift, and it becomes the choice of the recipient what they do with the gift. The truth is that this gift of salvation will not be available to you forever. James asks us, "How do you know what your life will be like tomorrow? Your life is like the morning fog—it's here a little while, then it's gone."[170] Once you pass into eternity, you will no longer be able to receive this gift.

I urge you to take this matter seriously. If you have not surrendered your life to Jesus Christ and received His gift of salvation, do not wait a moment longer. The Appendix at the back of this book provides simple directions on how to receive this amazing gift.

If you have this issue resolved in your heart and know that you will spend eternity with God, then you are ready to continue reading.

Blue-Sky Thinking

In the backdrop of Nehemiah's quest to rebuild the wall of Jerusalem, we find a story of great trials for God's people. Because of the sins and rebellion of God's people, they were exiled to Babylon. The Israelites were separated from their homeland, and over time they began to assimilate into their new land. They learned the local language and found employment with the Babylonians.

In Jeremiah chapter 28, a prophet named Hananiah rose to prominence by broadcasting "blue-sky" thinking. He proclaimed that within two years, the Israelites would be liberated and be able to return to their homeland. Hananiah gained quite a following, but not for long. The prophet Jeremiah exposed Hananiah as a false prophet before the people of God. He prophesied instead that Hananiah would meet an untimely end. This prophecy came true.[171]

Next, Jeremiah proclaimed what would really happen to the Israelites. In fact, there was more suffering to come. Let's pick up the story:

> "Go and tell Hananiah, 'This is what the LORD says: You have broken a wooden yoke, but in its place you will get a yoke of iron. This is what the LORD Almighty, the God of Israel, says: I will put an iron yoke on the necks of all these nations to make them serve Nebuchadnezzar king of Babylon, and they will serve him. I will even give him control over the wild animals.'" Then the prophet Jeremiah said to Hananiah the prophet, "Listen, Hananiah! The LORD has not sent you, yet you have persuaded this nation to trust in lies. Therefore this is what the LORD says: 'I am about to remove you from the face of the earth. This very year you are going to die, because you have preached rebellion against the LORD.'"[172]

We see here that Hananiah preached something that sounded like God, but wasn't God. One thing that puzzles Christ-followers and unbelievers alike is that when God speaks, sometimes He promises hardship. Jesus Himself said things like this: "Things that cause people to stumble are bound to come."[173] This does not look like what I saw in the brochure!

Then we have this story of someone approaching Jesus, hoping to become His follower:

> As they were walking along the road, a man said to him, "I will follow you wherever you go." Jesus replied, "Foxes have dens and birds have nests, but the Son of Man has no place to lay his head."[174]

This person probably meant well but was not prepared for what he heard. Don't forget, Jesus could read people's thoughts, and so He never needed to waste words.[175] God's plan is often not glamorous, but we arrive at a better place in the end. We are blessed when we trust God and take the high road.

What would you prefer? The freedom of an ugly reality, or the prison of a beautiful lie? If you are brave enough to let God into your real brokenness, your real struggles, and your real pain, the reality is better. Do not deceive yourself and those around you. It's not worth pretending that you're okay when you know deep down, you're really not. Do not settle for comfort. It may seem like a good option, but one day it could steal what is most precious to you—your faith. Before you invest in the stock market, make sure you invest in your faith. It is worth far more than gold.[176]

Let's revisit the story of Hananiah, the false prophet who made crowd-pleasing claims about the future. Was Jeremiah's message all doom-and-gloom? Not at all. After Hananiah was exposed in Jeremiah chapter 28, we see the famous declaration in Jeremiah 29:11—possibly one of the most-quoted verses in all of Scripture. This was what God wanted to say to His people—and also to you:

> This is what the LORD says: "When seventy years are completed for Babylon, I will come to you and fulfill my good promise to bring you back to this place. For I know the plans I have for you," declares the LORD, "plans to prosper you and not to harm you, plans to give you hope and a future. Then you will call on me and come and pray to me, and I will listen to you."[177]

Make sure you hold onto hope. I believe that God wants to say to you, "Don't worry. You may not understand what I'm doing right now, but trust Me." Instead of blue-sky thinking, embrace gray-sky thinking. This is not a worldview that says, "Nothing is going to go right." Rather, gray-sky thinking says, "Even if things go wrong, my God is greater than my problems. I never have to go through hard things alone."

Once upon a time, I had to make a hard life decision about whether to leave my hometown to study, or whether to stay local and find work. I knew God had a plan for me which would take me away from home, but the decision scared me. Then I saw this statement written by King Solomon:

> Whoever watches the wind will not plant; whoever looks at the clouds will not reap.[178]

I realized I was so in tune with my own life circumstances that I was out of tune with God. I was waiting for perfect circumstances to arrive before acting on what I knew God had told me to do. The same can be true of your life. Sure, there are sometimes unfavorable circumstances that can set you off-course or delay you, but what if there is nothing stopping you? Looking back, I know now that even if perfect circumstances came, I would not have started. God wants you to rise up and have the guts to start.

Envying the Wicked

When I was living in South Korea, God nourished me and built me up. Day after day, as I set aside time to spend with Him, God taught me things that I could never learn anywhere else. On one such occasion, the phrase, "do not envy the wicked" popped into my head. I found it in Psalm 37:

> Do not fret because of those who are evil or be envious of those who do wrong; for like the grass they will soon wither, like green plants they will soon die away.[179]

If you're like me, you have probably looked at some people that don't follow Christ and thought to yourself, "They don't seem to have many problems. I wish I had their life." This is bound to happen when you have unanswered questions, experience hurt at the hands of church people, or just find yourself in a difficult season. When this happens to you, don't forget—not every thought you have is necessarily your own. The enemy would love to convince you that following Jesus is not worth it. The enemy knows he is already on death row and so he will do anything to lure you away from God's salvation.

Fortunately, God provides us with a remedy. The next verse says:

> Trust in the LORD and do good; dwell in the land and enjoy safe pasture.[180]

If you want to get unstuck and build positive momentum in your life, start making some good decisions consistently. Start with one good decision. Then make another. Then another. After a while, you will see your momentum building. Some things in your life will begin to flow with ease. You will be able to tackle more difficult life issues. Your confidence will grow. And sooner or later, you will stop looking at what other people are doing.

There is a well-worn expression which goes like this: "The grass is always greener on the other side." I have heard a parody of this: "The grass is greener where you water it." Get excited about investing in your life, through the power of good choices. The bottom line is this: If you want to leave your past behind and embrace God's great plan for you, be prepared to do the work.

In Proverbs we see this powerful statement:

> Those who work their land will have abundant food, but those who chase fantasies will have their fill of poverty.[181]

Maybe you need to read that statement a few more times to let it sink in. Notice that when you chase fantasies, you will be repaid with poverty. Why? You are effectively telling yourself lies. Put your foot down and say "no" to fantasy—whether it be about a future spouse, job, or ministry. Am I saying it's not okay to want things? Not at all. But if you are stuck in fantasy mode, you are preventing God from working in your reality. Instead, let God heal your reality.

Did that burst your bubble? Were you hoping that God would bless your fantasy? I don't blame you. I've been there. But there is an even greater promise than enjoying safe pasture:

> Take delight in the Lord, and he will give you the desires of your heart.[182]

This is the path to fulfillment. Decide not to fixate on what people are doing around you, and start investing in your own life. Invest a little bit more each day. Brick by brick.

As you commit to doing this, God will meet you.[183] He is not a fantasy. He is real. As you step out, you may feel weak. But your weakness is a magnet for God's strength.[184] You may even feel bored. Embrace it. In the Bible, freedom is described as a "spacious place."[185] Give yourself a chance to adjust to your new normal.

Welcome to reality.

Building Blocks

- A sense of entitlement keeps you bound in passivity, indecision, and inaction.

- Victory begins when you forsake fantasy, and invite God into your reality.

- The path to fulfillment is a lifestyle of pleasing God.

14

ZEAL WITHOUT KNOWLEDGE
GET ACQUAINTED WITH GOD

Back in high school, I used to work at an electronics store on weekends. We sold everything from circuits to televisions, to video games. We also had a range of cell phones that probably belong in a museum. The uniform was black shoes, black trousers, a white business shirt, a black tie, and a bright yellow name tag. I had to dress like an absolute nerd.

We had a diverse demographic of customers. This gave me an opportunity to practice dealing with all kinds of people. Some people didn't know what a gigabyte is. Some resorted to profanity in the hope of getting faster service. Others didn't have a clue what they wanted. Others spoke with accents I could not understand, even if they spoke slowly. And the rest? They were just browsing.

I think I did okay overall. One of the survival skills I learned there was to walk around the store at the start of every shift. I was on the lookout for new products, which appeared on shelves regularly without warning. If I found something I'd never seen before, I would pick it up and read the back of the package. Most of the time I only knew slightly more than my customers did. If they asked me a technical question, the first thing I normally did was to read the package. After all, some customers weren't willing to do this for themselves, so I got away with this technique often.

Then, a day of reckoning came. A customer came in and asked me to show them the integrated circuits. I was thinking to myself, "Integrated what?" I knew so little about electronics that my customers had to teach me. My customers basically taught me everything I know about electronics—which is still not much. I was always just getting by. Hey, at least I kept smiling, right?

There are plenty of Christ-followers like this. They are pumped, excited, amped—or pick your favorite adjective. Like me in the electronics store, these people can quote Bible verses from memory, they know the words to the songs, and they even volunteer. But they have only taken the time to read the "package" of God and never really opened it up.

Progress with the Wall

In the story of Nehemiah, we witness a scene in which the wall reaches half height. The battle was far from over. Meanwhile, Nehemiah's enemies were hatching a plot to sabotage the wall and stop the construction. Let's pick up the story:

> So we rebuilt the wall till all of it reached half its height, for the people worked with all their heart.
>
> But when Sanballat, Tobiah, the Arabs, the Ammonites and the people of Ashdod heard that the repairs to Jerusalem's walls had gone ahead and that the gaps were being closed, they were very angry. They all plotted together to come and fight against Jerusalem and stir up trouble

against it. But we prayed to our God and posted a guard day and night to meet this threat.

Meanwhile, the people in Judah said, "The strength of the laborers is giving out, and there is so much rubble that we cannot rebuild the wall."[186]

Notice that the wall was at half height. This was a big achievement for Nehemiah, but the wall was still not high enough to keep the baddies out. Think of this as a picture of your life. If you build a life that is only sustained by passion and excitement, you will have limited protection against the thoughts that can bring you down. You might be fine for a while, but, eventually, you will run out of strength and be overcome. To finish your "wall," you need knowledge—and not just any knowledge. You need the "knowledge of God."

Knowledge is Critical

Jesus told a parable about a farmer who was sowing seed. Some seed fell on the path, some on the rocks, some among thorns, and some on good soil. Jesus pulled back the curtain and explained to us what this means. The seed on the path represents people who do not understand God's message. The seed on the rocks speaks of those who are excited about God's message, but they have shallow roots: when trouble comes, they wither. The seed among thorns represents people who are lured away by the "worries of this life and deceitfulness of wealth." Finally, the seed in good soil represents the kind of person I know you want to be: it grows and produces a huge harvest.[187] People like this are fiercely determined to know God, and they are the ones who will end up living by His truth.

What is the knowledge of God? Simply put, it is *knowing God*. We know that Moses spoke with God like a friend.[188] God is a person. In fact, you are made in God's image.[189] This means that in many ways, God created you to be a scale model of Him. You are not an accident.

To understand how critical the knowledge of God is to your success, you need to see how aggressively the enemy tries to undermine it. The Apostle Paul writes:

> We demolish arguments and every pretension that sets itself up against the knowledge of God, and we take captive every thought to make it obedient to Christ.[190]

The world you live in is full of arguments and pretensions. People go to great lengths to deny the existence of God, the character of God, or the authority of God. The enemy likes to play "mind games" with humanity, to deceive, seduce, and take people captive.

For this reason, you must pursue the knowledge of God like your very life depends on it. The book of Proverbs has plenty to tell us about the fear of God. Simply put, knowing God is to fear God, and the fear of God makes you wise. We read in Proverbs that "[the] fear of the Lord is the beginning of wisdom, and knowledge of the Holy One is understanding."[191] This is not a fear that makes you "scared" of God. It is a fear that keeps you close to Him, and away from danger. It is a fear that drives you toward Him. Being seated in heavenly places with Him is the safest place in the universe.[192] We are told elsewhere in Proverbs, "The fear of the Lord leads to life; then one rests content, untouched by trouble."[193] If you want to be wise, and you want to endure until the end, invest time in getting to know God.

Zeal Without Knowledge

Just to be clear, I am not "anti-passion." Passion is often how things get started. Passion is often what makes life feel like it's worth living. Passion is essential for thriving relationships, and for reaching any of your goals in life. But know this: you need both passion and knowledge, so you can be a well-rounded person who will stand strong and weather the storms of life.

The Apostle Paul knew well the plight of the Israelites in Nehemiah's day. Before his radical encounter with Jesus, Paul was called Saul. He was a Pharisee: a devout Jew with high standing in his religious sect. He thought the best way to please God was to hunt down Christians and throw them in jail. On the contrary, after his encounter with Jesus on the road to Damascus,[194] he became the most influential missionary of all time. Once influential among the Jews, he became an outsider. Here are his thoughts about his former brethren:

> For I can testify about them that they are zealous for God, but their zeal is not based on knowledge. Brothers and sisters, my heart's desire and prayer to God for the Israelites is that they may be saved. Since they did not know the righteousness of God and sought to establish their own, they did not submit to God's righteousness. Christ is the culmination of the law so that there may be righteousness for everyone who believes.[195]

In the Bible, God frequently uses the Israelites as an example to us regarding the ways of humanity, and our tendency to drift from God. Proverbs puts it this way: "Desire without knowledge is not good—how much more will hasty feet miss the way!"[196]

Passion is Not Enough

It is dangerous for you to think that as long as you do the visible things well, then you will have a great relationship with God and you will not stumble. So, what should you do about it? In this section, let's unpack some key ways you can develop the knowledge of God in your own life.

Pray

I like to think of "prayer" as a fancy word for "conversation with God." Don't complicate it. When you talk with God as with a friend, you'll find yourself increasingly enjoying His company. In the beginning, this may seem like small talk, "How's the weather?" In time you will begin to feel safe in His Presence. You'll notice I did not say talk *to* God but rather talk *with* God. You may be wondering how on earth God talks back. He does talk back; it is just not necessarily with an audible voice. One common way that God speaks is like a whisper.[197] Another common way God speaks is through people, and, occasionally, through circumstances. Having said that, make sure you check everything you hear against the Word of God—the Bible. That is His fingerprint on earth. If what you heard contradicts the Word of God, discard it.[198] Most of all, be patient. You need to play the long game.

Read

My favorite book in the world is the Bible, which I believe is the Word of God. Why? Because through the Bible I have come to know the Creator of the Universe. He not only cared enough about us to send Jesus to die for our sins, but He arranged for all this amazing truth to be recorded in book form. The Bible we know is made up of sixty-six "books" of various genres, but God breathed His inspiration on all of it. The Apostle Paul tells us:

> All Scripture is God-breathed and is useful for teaching, rebuking, correcting and training in righteousness, so that the servant of God may be thoroughly equipped for every good work.[199]

How on earth can you get to know God by reading a book? Just ask my wife, Cherie. Her first time meeting Jesus was not within the four walls of a church. A friend of hers had recently met Jesus and told Cherie all about her experience. She told Cherie how much God loves her. Cherie went to a bookstore close by, found a "Holy Bible" on the shelf, bought it, and proceeded to read it cover-to-cover in three months. And, get this: English is her second language. If that's not passion, I don't know what is. This passion birthed the breathtaking knowledge of God she shows today.

Read the Bible. You may feel overwhelmed by the number of different translations available. You will also hear people criticize various translations. Don't get hung up on these arguments. As I have heard it said, "The best Bible translation is the one you read." Pure and simple. The Bible is most beneficial to your life when you read it. Get one that you find easy to read, and then get started. Read a little bit every day. If you don't understand what you're reading, ask God to help you understand. Then ask someone you trust to explain things to you.

By investing a little bit of time every day, you are programming yourself with God's thoughts, and His worldview. And, by the way, there are many resources in bookstores and online which can help you understand the Bible better. Most importantly, make sure you start today and get to know God more accurately.

Worship

You were created for a relationship with God. The only logical response to knowing God is to worship Him. Practically speaking, there are a few ways to easily make this part of your life. It can be as simple as shutting the bedroom door, playing some worship music, and taking the time to sing to your Creator. Sometimes you may just wait in God's presence and find refreshment. Don't forget though: Worship is not just a thing you do sometimes—it is a lifestyle.

The Apostle Paul explains it like this:

So here's what I want you to do, God helping you: Take your everyday, ordinary life—your sleeping, eating, going-to-work, and walking-around life—and place it before God as an offering. Embracing what God does for you is the best thing you can do for him.[200]

The best way to build a relationship with God is to give Him *you*. Give Him your time and attention. Give Him your everyday life. Let Him spend time with you, no matter what you're doing.

In all three of the disciplines above, the result is getting to know God better. Just like any close relationship, I encourage you to give up your "fantasy self" and be your "real self" before God. You do not need to pretend or role-play before God. Ask Him questions, and express your doubts. He is not intimidated in the slightest by your unbelief. He is the best friend you will ever have in your life. Invest in getting to know God better.

You'll thank me later.

Building Blocks

- Passion for God is not enough; you need the knowledge of God.
- The fear of God is a healthy fear. It keeps you close to Him.
- The knowledge of God enables you to live a Spirit-led life.

15

THE UNSEALED LETTER
TRUST HIM AT ALL TIMES

Resistance

If you choose to follow Christ, you will face resistance. It comes in many forms—visible, invisible, tangible, and intangible. Note that it can come through people, but is not *from* people. This is an important distinction. People themselves are not the source of this resistance. The Apostle Paul tells us that, "... our struggle is not against flesh and blood, but against the rulers, against the authorities, against the powers of this dark world and against the spiritual forces of evil in the heavenly realms."[201]

If you are facing opposition or resistance, it may not always be obvious. Allow me to give you some examples. Getting things done can be more difficult than normal. Your mind might be plagued with unclean and fearful thoughts. A family member that is usually healthy suddenly gets sick. It can manifest in so many ways. I implore you not to give up. Stand your ground.

Bad Day?

Please hear me; this is not about becoming paranoid. Don't forget that God is on the throne. If you fear Him, you don't need to fear anyone or anything else. However, as we discussed earlier, not every thought you have is your own. You certainly don't want to accept every thought that comes into your mind.

In case you didn't know, you have an enemy. This enemy does not want you to think clearly, to worship God, or to please God in any way. He knows that if you do, then you will take territory from him. Before Jesus went to the cross and won the ultimate victory for us, He called the enemy "the prince of this world," saying:

> I have told you now before it happens, so that when it does happen you will believe. I will not say much more to you, for the prince of this world is coming. He has no hold over me, but he comes so that the world may learn that I love the Father and do exactly what my Father has commanded me.[202]

Whenever you live in a way that truly pleases God, you are taking territory from the prince of this world. Can you see now why the enemy would want to stop you? Be encouraged, friend. In the same breath, Jesus tells us that this prince has no hold on Him. If Jesus could proclaim that in His darkest hour, then so can you. Let these words of Jesus encourage you today:

> '... In this world you will have trouble. But take heart! I have overcome the world.'[203]

If you have given your life over to Jesus, then you have become a child of God. You are now an overcomer. It is in your DNA.

Distraction

Now let's look at one of the primary tactics used against God's people—distraction.

In the book of Nehemiah, we see Nehemiah approached by his enemies. Interestingly, at this time, the wall of Jerusalem had been completed, and the Bible tells us that there was not a gap left in it. All that remained were the city gates.[204] At this point, Sanballat and Geshem heard the news and started a new campaign against Nehemiah.

Sanballat and Geshem worked diligently to distract Nehemiah from his mission. They invited him four times to meet them in the valley of Ono. It was clearly a trap. When they made the same invitation to Nehemiah for the fifth time, they sent their aide with an unsealed letter. Nehemiah tells the story like this:

> ... the fifth time, Sanballat sent his aide to me with the same message, and in his hand was an unsealed letter in which was written: "It is reported among the nations—and Geshem says it is true—that you and the Jews are plotting to revolt, and therefore you are building the wall. Moreover, according to these reports you are about to become their king and have even appointed prophets to make this proclamation about you in Jerusalem: 'There is a king in Judah!' Now this report will get back to the king; so come, let us meet together."[205]

The letter was laced with half-truths to discredit Nehemiah and his fellow Israelites. But notice that Nehemiah's resolve to complete the wall was so strong, not even this unsealed letter could throw him. The Bible is a living book, and there is no insignificant detail. Nehemiah tells us that the letter was unsealed. This tells me that the letter, though scary in its content, lacked any real authority. This is similar to a dream I had in Osaka, Japan, which I will explain in the next chapter. Just as Nehemiah held his ground, I refused to give the dream any power over me.

Know this: the enemy has already lost the war. He has no authority over you if you are in Christ. His position is weak. The Bible promises that if we submit to God and resist the devil, he will flee from us.[206] Keep your eyes fixed on Jesus, and focus on pleasing Him.

Use Your Hands

Nehemiah stood his ground. Watch how he responded:

> They were all trying to frighten us, thinking, "Their hands will get too weak for the work, and it will not be completed." But I prayed, "Now strengthen my hands."[207]

I believe that Nehemiah asking God to strengthen his hands was more than a physical thing. Elsewhere in the Bible, we see many references to the hands. What else did people use their hands for?

Praise.

In the book of Psalms, we read statements like this: "Lift up your hands in the sanctuary and praise the LORD."[208] We are also told how God equips us to live successfully to please Him. King David wrote:

> He makes my feet like the feet of a deer,
> He causes me to stand on the heights.
> He trains my hands for battle,
> So that my arms can bend a bow of bronze.[209]

Your hands are not just for hard work. They are weapons of praise. When you lift your hands to God in praise, you cannot do work at the same time. You are making Him your focus, and reminding yourself that God is your source of everything. When praise is coming out of your mouth, negativity just can't come out at the same time. You are showing your soul, and your mouth, who's boss!

When you are confronted with lies and threats, no matter how real they seem, do what James instructs us to do: "Submit yourselves, then, to God. Resist the devil, and he will flee from you. Come near to God, and he will come near to you . . ."[210] Do not neglect to praise your King. When you praise God, you invite Him into your situation, and He becomes your strength. He gives you the ability to stand against all the odds.

The Hospital

Maybe you cannot think of something that could easily identify as an unsealed letter in your life. What about a more physical example? Here is a story of how praise and thankfulness changed the atmosphere.

Years ago, when my wife was about to give birth for the first time, I found myself in a hospital in South Korea, waiting nervously for the baby to come. My wife's labor pains began before noon, and they went on. And on. Before long, the sun was sinking behind the horizon. The hospital ward was becoming increasingly quiet. The ward resembled an emergency room, and the layout was much like an aircraft carrier. The mothers-to-be waited for their turn to be whisked into the operating room. The whole time I kept praying to God and thanking Him.

We were fortunate enough to have an English-speaking doctor. She explained to me that the chances of a normal delivery had become slim. I chose to have faith, and I simply responded with, "Thank you." In the end, after a lot of doubting and a lot of pain, our daughter was born at just after two in the morning. No emergency surgery was required.

A day or two later, I happened to meet that doctor in the cafe on the ground floor of the hospital. I took the opportunity to thank her for everything she did that night: "Doctor, in that hospital room were the two most important people to me in the whole world, and you took great care of them. Thank you so much."

The doctor replied, "You know, normally new parents don't listen to my instructions. They tend to complain a lot and never say 'thank you.' But you two did both these things. What is different about you?" I was able to share with her about my faith in Christ.

This was an unforgettable moment. God showed Himself strong in a difficult situation. The enemy will try to convince you that nothing good can come of your pain. Keep your attitude of gratitude. Not only will it affect your life, but it will spill over to other people—like our doctor.

Bricks and Mortar

We have talked in this book about a lot of the bricks that you need in order to see continued growth and momentum in your life. There is one thing though that I strongly believe helps you maintain the growth and momentum you already have. Belief is important, and perseverance in hard times is important, but unless you have this next component, you will struggle with momentum.

Praise is the very mortar which binds your wall together. Depending on your background, the word praise may invoke vastly different images. The bottom line is that you thank God for who He is, and what He has done. When you do this, it's almost as if God gets *bigger*. Not that He isn't big already, but when you praise God, you give Him more real estate in your heart, and your perspective begins to shift.

I am not only interested in the act of praise itself, but in a lifestyle of praise that helps you to overcome the "unsealed letters" in your life. Let's dive in.

The Power of PRAISE

Here are some benefits that praise will bring to your life:

1) **P**erspective on your Challenges

2) **R**efreshing for your Soul

3) **A**ssurance of Salvation

4) **I**mpartation of Faith

5) **S**trength to Persevere

6) **E**xpansion of your Territory

Perspective on Your Challenges

A lifestyle of praising God maintains your ability to see the "big picture" of your life. If you can see Jesus and what He's done, you can overcome in situations that would otherwise cause you to give up. Your focus will make or break you in the midst of a trial. As Paul directed Timothy:

> You then, my son, be strong in the grace that is in Christ Jesus. And the things you have heard me say in the presence of many witnesses entrust to reliable people who will also be qualified to teach others. Join with me in suffering, like a good soldier of Christ Jesus. No one serving as a soldier gets entangled in civilian affairs, but rather tries to please his commanding officer.[211]

Praise keeps your focus directed towards the One you ultimately want to please. Similarly, we read in Scripture, "As the eyes of slaves look to the hand of their master, as the eyes of a female slave look to the hand of her mistress, so our eyes look to the LORD our God, till he shows us his mercy."[212]

When the Arameans came to hunt down Elisha in the Old Testament, Elisha's servant awoke in great alarm to see their camp surrounded by hostile troops. Elisha simply addressed his servant's perspective:

> "Don't be afraid," the prophet answered. "Those who are with us are more than those who are with them."[213]

When you are walking closely with God and your focus is on Him, you can see that you have the victory. While there is no direct mention in the Bible of Elisha praising God, you can see from the way He talks that God is at the center of Elisha's game plan. God is his quarterback.

> And Elisha prayed, "Open his eyes, LORD, so that he may see." Then the LORD opened the servant's eyes, and he looked and saw the hills full of horses and chariots of fire all around Elisha.[214]

Praise opens your eyes to see things you could not see before.

Rest and Refreshing for Your Soul

Praise can refresh you. In the Psalms we read:

> Return to your rest, my soul, for the LORD has been good to you. For you, LORD, have delivered me from death, my eyes from tears, my feet from stumbling, that I may walk before the LORD in the land of the living.[215]

Praise needs to be a part of your everyday life. Praise takes you from being in an "I'm on my own" mindset to a "God is for me" mindset. Christ died for you and me so that we could enjoy the gifts of forgiveness, cleansing, and freedom in Him. The writer of Hebrews unpacks for us the importance of accepting the work of Christ. It is about what He does for us—and whatever we do for Him does not justify us but is just a response to His goodness. Let's read this powerful passage:

> There remains, then, a Sabbath-rest for the people of God; for anyone who enters God's rest also rests from their works, just as God did from his. Let us, therefore, make every effort to enter that rest, so that no one will perish by following their example of disobedience.[216]

To be refreshed, then, it is essential to remember the finished work of Jesus Christ on the cross of Calvary. Because of the cross, we always have something to praise God for. Lastly, Isaiah wrote these words:

> [God] gives strength to the weary and increases the power of the weak. Even youths grow tired and weary, and young men stumble and fall; but those who hope in the LORD will renew their strength. They will soar on wings like eagles; they will run and not grow weary, they will walk and not be faint.[217]

So get busy thanking Him.

Assurance of Salvation

You may not realize this, but often the enemy will try to maneuver you into an identity crisis. When he was tempting Jesus in the desert, he said, "If you are the Son of God, tell these stones to become bread."[218] Jesus had no doubt in His mind that He was the Son of God. He knew He had nothing to prove, yet the devil requested that Jesus prove Himself. Think about it for a moment. In light of what we discussed in Part 2 of this book, can anything change your identity in Christ? No. Yet you may find yourself coming under feelings of condemnation again. Maybe you made a mistake. Maybe something completely unexpected happened in your life, such as losing a job or falling ill.

This is a key area in which you need to stay strong at all times. Fortunately, praise can help. Paul wrote:

> Therefore, brothers and sisters, since we have confidence to enter the Most Holy Place by the blood of Jesus, by a new and living way opened for us through the curtain, that is, his body, and since we have a great priest over the house of God, let us draw near to God with a sincere heart and with the full assurance that faith brings, having our hearts sprinkled to cleanse us from a guilty conscience and having our bodies washed with pure water. And by that will, we have been made holy through the sacrifice of the body of Jesus Christ once for all. Let us hold unswervingly to the hope we profess, for he who promised is faithful.[219]

Impartation of Faith

King David gives us the following insight into praise:

> He put a new song in my mouth, a hymn of praise to our God. Many will see and fear the LORD and put their trust in him.[220]

Praise not only builds your faith, but it can also build the faith of others. It does something powerful in the spiritual realm. To illustrate this point, let's look at a story from the life of Moses. This story occurs after he had brought the people of God out of Egypt. During the Israelites' battle with the

Amalekites, he went to an elevated position and raised his hands. As long as he kept his hands up in a posture of praise, the Israelites kept winning, but as soon as he started lowering his hands, the Amalekites began to win.[221] Moses was now an old man, and his arms grew weak. Two of his attendants came to his aid. Together they held up Moses' arms, and so the Israelites proceeded to win the battle.

Don't try to fight the fight of faith on your own. God responds to your faith. Take people with you on the journey wherever possible. We are stronger when we praise God together. Just like Moses did, make sure you surround yourself with people who can pray with you, believe with you, and stand with you during these moments of resistance. Let's read the rest of the story:

> When Moses' hands grew tired, [Aaron and Hur] took a stone and put it under him and he sat on it. Aaron and Hur held his hands up—one on one side, one on the other—so that his hands remained steady till sunset. So Joshua overcame the Amalekite army with the sword.[222]

Strength to Persevere

Praise builds your faith and allows joy to manifest in your life. The Bible tells us that true joy is found in God's presence.[223] When I speak of joy, I am referring to the positive energy that comes from the Spirit of God. The main difference between joy and happiness is that happiness comes from our environment, but joy comes from God. Joy is supernatural. Nehemiah himself told his people that "the joy of the LORD is [their] strength."[224]

Encouragement When You Most Need It

Gideon was given the daunting assignment of defeating the fearsome Midianite army. When we first read about Gideon, he is introduced to us as a disillusioned and timid man. Amazingly, God shows His incredible Father-heart for us in the way He encourages Gideon for this assignment. Let's follow the story:

> During that night the Lord said to Gideon, "Get up, go down against the camp, because I am going to give it into your hands. If you are afraid to attack, go down to the camp with your servant Purah and listen to what they are saying. Afterward, you will be encouraged to attack the camp." So he and Purah his servant went down to the outposts of the camp. The Midianites, the Amalekites and all the other eastern peoples had settled in the valley, thick as locusts. Their camels could no more be counted than the sand on the seashore. Gideon arrived just as a man was telling a friend his dream. "I had a dream," he was saying. "A round loaf of barley bread came tumbling into the Midianite camp. It struck the tent with such force that the tent overturned and collapsed." His friend responded, "This can be nothing other than the sword of Gideon son of Joash, the Israelite. God has given the Midianites and the whole camp into his hands."[225]

Wow. Gideon was afraid of the Midianites. But the Midianites were even more afraid of Gideon and his God. If we fix our attention and affection on God, He has the power to change our perspective, displace our anxiety, and to encourage us in a way that nobody else can.

In closing, your God is stronger than anything you will ever come against. Set your mind on Him. Nothing can stop Him. He overcame the world.

Building Blocks

- There is a real enemy who authors real resistance in your life.

- If you live a life that pleases God, you will end up taking territory from the enemy.

- Praise keeps you dependent on God and helps you win the battle.

16

THE CITY GATES
GUARD YOUR HEART

The Warning in My Dream

In my high school days, there was a girl I was interested in. I was unprepared for my feelings, and I could not even concentrate in math class. This went on for weeks. Then, one night, I had a dream.

It was night. I was standing near a suburban house. This same girl climbed into an old, deep yellow car with her family to drive away. I called out to her to say hello, but none of them seemed to notice. Then, as the car rolled away, I noticed there were five or six small puppies scurrying around in the back window.

I woke up. At the time, I had no idea what this dream meant, but it was unforgettable. A year or two later, I came to understand that dogs can represent a backsliding spirit. I realized that a deep relationship with this girl could pull me away from God. You know what I did? I let her go. To this day, I believe that God spared me the pain of that relationship. Experiences like this one helped prepare me for the marriage relationship I enjoy today.

In my earlier years, I thought that God was somehow letting me down. After all, He didn't let me have what I wanted. I know better now. I recognize that God wants to be close to me. As part of that, He wants me to learn how to guard my heart. There are so many things out there that can bring us down. Guarding your heart is so important that Proverbs boldly says:

> Above all else, guard your heart, for everything you do flows from it.[226]

Everything flows from your heart. I hope you are not just exposing yourself to any influence. You need to guard your heart as if your life depends on it.

Osaka

I remember a time when I was on tour with a worship band in Japan. We were just past the halfway mark in the tour. We had already seen amazing things happen and were excited about the event in the next city. In Osaka, we saw many people believe in Christ for the first time in their lives. In a country where believing in Christ can mean rejection by family, this moment is life-defining in every way imaginable.

That night in Osaka, I had a dream. A world-renowned church leader was brought onto the stage of a TV show and ridiculed. This leader was walking awkwardly like he was drunk. The crowd was cheering. I woke up. It was the middle of the night. I felt a sense of terror: this dream was not from God.

I began to pace the corridor of the dormitory where we were staying. I prayed and prayed until the heaviness lifted.

Eventually, I got back to sleep. The next day, we went to our next destination. We had yet another breakthrough night, with many people giving their lives to Christ. Had I not been consistently walking with God, that dream could have completely derailed me.

So how do you guard your heart? You need discernment.

The last time we checked on Nehemiah, the walls were complete, which meant that the city had protection again. But one thing was missing: the gates.[227] Though the city was now less vulnerable, there was still not much stopping outsiders from coming in and plundering the city.

Your ability to discern is like a pair of city gates. We see that the walls of Jerusalem had been burned.[228] Just as the city needed new gates, you must develop the skill of discernment. In a world where we are presented with so many options—so many ideologies, products, and techniques—it is a great comfort to me to know that we are not alone when we make choices. In fact, the Prophet Isaiah talks about how God helps us in decision making. He wrote:

> Whether you turn to the right or to the left, your ears will hear a voice behind you, saying, "This is the way; walk in it."[229]

So set your mind to involve God in your life decisions. I am not talking about what to have for lunch today, although I am certain He can help with that decision also. I am talking about who you should spend your time with, what movies you should watch, what music to listen to, and so on. Your heart is more important than friendships, and entertainment.

Who's in Charge?

There was a time in my life where I was a bit bored. I wanted to spice things up a bit. In hindsight, this was because I didn't know what I am about to teach you. There were plenty of people in Bible times who worshipped other gods. I wondered what they were all up to in the 21st century. Curiosity got the better of me. In hindsight, this was not a great research topic. Sure, I did find some interesting information on the Internet. There are even plenty of these people who now follow Christ.

This study seemed harmless at the beginning, but it had quite a negative effect on my mind. This is an example of me failing at discernment. I started to feel afraid all the time. For weeks, I was even afraid of the dark. If I wanted to simply get a glass of water late at night, I had to turn all the lights on in my house. This was not normal for me. I had inadvertently exposed myself to something spiritual.

This experience went on for weeks. I prayed to God to take this "thing" away. Then one day, I traveled to another city to visit extended family. I went outside and looked up at the stars. My mind was the clearest it had been in months. I asked the Holy Spirit, "How do I overcome this darkness?" Within seconds, He reminded me of a Bible verse I had read several times. This time it carried a powerful punch:

> All authority in heaven and on earth has been given to [Jesus Christ].[230]

I had my answer. In the weeks following, every time I had a dark or fearful thought, I spoke the Word of God: "All authority in heaven and on earth has been given to [Jesus Christ]." Before long, my mind was clear again, and I have not struggled with those same thoughts since. This remains one of my favorite verses to this day. It reminds me that no matter what is going on, Jesus is still on the throne.

This revelation about the authority of Jesus Christ has been powerful in my life. I believe that if you proclaim this truth, you too can keep your mind clear, and live a life of serial victory over dark thoughts. But please, don't do what I did and go looking for trouble. Keep your eyes fixed on Jesus at all times, and focus on pleasing Him. That's all you need to do.

The Preacher

Several years ago, I was enamoured with a certain preacher. He was in high demand as a visiting speaker. One night, he was preaching at a church nearby. He started with some anecdotes about his everyday life. Then he launched into his message. I leaned in with great anticipation. The things he said were not unusual, but I had this sense that something was not right. I felt strangely uncomfortable the whole time he was speaking.

I doubted myself a little at the time. I thought, maybe I just wasn't "spiritually mature" enough to understand what he was saying. Yet this experience lingered with me.

Sadly, I heard some news not long after this event. Apparently, this same man resigned from his ministry because of issues in his personal life. I feel compassion for this man. He was a powerful man of God. Sadly, this kind of experience is quite common in the Church. Even the most anointed and talented person can be derailed from his or her God-given purpose. Issues in your inner life can grow like weeds if you are not vigilant. Look at King Solomon. God made him the wisest king in all of human history,[231] yet towards the end of his life, his heart turned away from God and toward idols.[232]

Still, all this begs the question: what was it that made me feel uncomfortable when the preacher was speaking? Looking back, I now realize that this "red flag" I had on the inside was a God-given gift of discernment. Jesus tells us that whatever attitudes are in your heart will eventually come out of your mouth.[233] What happened to this man could easily happen to you or me. If you do not have a filter on your ears, your mind, and your heart, you can easily be derailed by the words and deeds of other people, or by your circumstances. The Apostle

Paul tells us to test everything and hold onto what is good.[234] If you belong to Christ, you too can cultivate discernment. The easiest way to do this is to spend time with God—every day, if you can. Read the Bible. Pray. Listen to Him. Jesus talks about Himself as a shepherd: "My sheep listen to my voice. I know them, and they follow me."[235] How can you know His voice if He's a stranger to you? Get to know Him. He is worth it.

Programmed for Victory

Before we wrap up this book, I want to share with you one of the most powerful principles I have ever learned from the Bible. It is this: your mind works in much the same way as a computer (not that computers existed in Bible times). Just as a computer can accept software, your brain can be programmed through the worldview and beliefs you adopt. God spoke this powerful truth through the Apostle Paul:

> I urge you, brothers and sisters, in view of God's mercy, to offer your bodies as a living sacrifice, holy and pleasing to God—this is your true and proper worship. Do not conform to the pattern of this world, but be transformed by the renewing of your mind. Then you will be able to test and approve what God's will is—his good, pleasing and perfect will.[236]

The secret to growth is to renew your mind. If you take a rough rock, and you put it in a river or stream, the rock will become smooth over time due to the friction from the flowing water. These smooth stones can kill giants. Just ask King David about his run-in with Goliath.[237] In the same way, repeated exposure to the Word of God will change you from the inside out, and make you into a weapon in God's hands.

You may struggle to dedicate time to read the Bible or listen to good teaching. Perhaps think about what other media you are consuming. Try swapping out the world's word—with God's Word.

There is another key benefit of renewing your mind: you can test and approve what God's will is. That sounds like discernment to me. How would you like to know what God wants you to do with your life? Start by spending time in His Word, and applying the principles highlighted in this book. Keep doing it. God might not tell you every detail, and so be open to that. Instead, expect that He will love you every step of the way.

Building Blocks

- Guarding your heart is something only you can do.

- All authority in heaven and on earth has been given to Jesus Christ.

- Renewing your mind is the best way to learn discernment and make wise decisions.

CONCLUSION
OUR ENEMY TREMBLES

The wall is complete, but the journey continues

The sky was a deep blue that day. The sound of rejoicing could be heard as the people of Israel inserted the final bricks in the wall. Three. Two. One. Shouts of joy erupted as the final brick slid into place. The people shouted even louder as the gates closed for the first time. The work was complete.

The wall gleamed beneath the fierce Middle Eastern sun. The strong wall of weathered and burnt bricks towered above the people. The gates were strong and glorious to behold. The people of God could once again dwell in safety. The story of this victory would be told for hundreds of years to come.

Did this mean that there was no longer a threat of enemy attack? Certainly not. Did it mean that the Israelites could rest on their laurels and become complacent? No way. Rather, it signified to the Israelites, and all the peoples settled around

CONCLUSION

them, that the tables had turned. Fear struck the enemies of Israel, like a tsunami. Nehemiah brings us this powerful conclusion:

> So the wall was completed on the twenty-fifth of Elul, in fifty-two days. When all our enemies heard about this, all the surrounding nations were afraid and lost their self-confidence, because they realized that this work had been done with the help of our God.[238]

The journey was not over for the people of Israel. It is also not over for you and me. Far from it, friend. Keep developing a deep and vital relationship with God. Help others build their walls. Become the kind of person that lives for Jesus, and then, from a position of strength, turns and lives for others.

I trust that God has spoken to you as you have taken this journey with me. I urge you to take the next step. Take action, even if it seems unspiritual. Little by little, you will begin to sense the protection of His walls and experience a life that is anything *but* ordinary.

APPENDIX
BELIEVING IN JESUS

What must you do to be saved and live eternally with God in Heaven? According to the Bible, you must believe in Jesus and make Him your Master. The Apostle Paul puts it this way:

> Say the welcoming word to God—"Jesus is my Master"—embracing, body and soul, God's work of doing in us what he did in raising Jesus from the dead. That's it. You're not "doing" anything; you're simply calling out to God, trusting him to do it for you. That's salvation. With your whole being you embrace God setting things right, and then you say it, right out loud: "God has set everything right between him and me!"[239]

Perhaps you have never consciously accepted Jesus as your Master, or perhaps over time, you have begun to doubt that you belong to Him. In any case, please pray this prayer from your heart:

> *"Jesus, I believe in my heart and confess with my mouth that You died on the cross to forgive my sin, and You rose from the dead. Please forgive me, cleanse me, and make me new. You are now my Master. Thank You, Jesus."*

If you made the decision to believe in Jesus and prayed the above prayer from your heart, congratulations! You are now a new creation in Christ,[240] and you have "passed from death to life."[241] Start involving Jesus in every area of your life. Follow His lead. You will not regret it.

I challenge you to tell someone about the great decision you have made. If you cannot tell your family, perhaps tell a friend who believes in Jesus. Find a church leader who can help you take the next steps in your relationship with Jesus.

I would love to hear from you and celebrate your wonderful decision. Reach me via my website: *StuartLamont.me*.

ACKNOWLEDGEMENTS

My name may be on the front of the book, but it could not have been written without the support of these people. While it is difficult to name everyone I am grateful for, the following people stand out.

Cherie Lamont: You supported me throughout this project, even long before there was a book. I am grateful to God that I am paired with a woman who closely shares my values. I couldn't imagine doing life with anybody else. I love you.

Lois and Phoebe Lamont: You are my baby girls. Both of you bring sunshine into my life. Thanks for putting up with Daddy while he wrote his book. Let's go to the beach again soon.

Richard Lamont: Dad—as I was growing up, you prayed for me every night, asking God to make me wise. Without your prayers, I would have nothing to write. Thank you for sacrificially investing in me for decades.

Janelle Lamont: Mom—you told me for years that I could write. You also modeled the importance of serving the body of Christ—His church. Your fingerprints are forever on my story.

Cameron Lamont: I'm grateful for the way you seek to add value to me, especially in recent times. You are one of the most determined people I know. Keep adding value to people.

Gordon and Eunice Frazer: To my beloved grandparents. You modeled to me what it is to serve God, and serve my family, day in and day out, for a lifetime. Your love remains a strong pillar in my heritage. I cherish our memories together. Pa—you passed away one year before I started writing this book, but I know you would have been proud of me. Ma—I look forward to placing this book in your hands.

Samuel McNamara: You came along at the right time and taught me how to be a friend.

Ps Samuel Lim: I would not be where I am today without your companionship, our long deep-and-meaningful conversations in the car, and your unwavering belief in me.

Mark Heywood: You're like a pillar in my life. Thank you for simply being there.

Chris Heyward: You taught me the power of being myself. Thank you for helping to shape the development of the manuscript early on with your trademark enthusiasm.

Aaron and Judith Guilmette: Over the past decade, it's been a privilege to share life with you. When we are together, I remember God's goodness.

Tommy Leonard: I cannot forget the feeling when I attended the launch of your first book. A seed was planted in my soul that day—and now I am beholding a "tree" of my own.

Ps Rod Plummer: Soaking in the culture of your church for one year taught me the power of acceptance, and convinced me that anything is possible with God.

ACKNOWLEDGEMENTS

Kary Oberbrunner and the Igniting Souls Tribe: Thank you for believing in me. True to your mission, you have ignited my soul so that I can share my message with the world.

Mary Valloni, Terry Stafford, Amy Hooke, and Shelly Snow Pordea—my mastermind group: You armed me with the self-awareness and confidence I needed to take the leap into authordom.

Elizabeth Hoa Nguyễn: Thank you for showing me the power of clarity, accountability, and the importance of shared vision. I got unstuck and made it to the finish line because of you.

Teri Capshaw—my editor: Your passion for God—and for the written word—shine through on this project. Thank you for getting behind the vision of BUILD.

Martyn Wood: You came to me at a time in the writing process when I was unsure if this message would resonate on paper. I was astounded by the depth at which you understood the message. Your encouragement and prayer in this time have been like jet fuel.

Nanette O'Neal: Your kind words during the final stages of writing helped me disembark from the emotional rollercoaster and stand firm until the last word was written.

Terry Stafford: Your support and your ministry example have been invaluable in my quest to produce a literary work I can be proud of.

Joan Turley: From the moment we met, you have been a deep well of encouragement for me. Thank you for taking an interest in me, and in BUILD.

Mary Valloni: Thank you for being a truth teller during this process. Watching you keep a sweet spirit and operate in your God-given calling inspires me to be better in my own life.

Eric Eaton: You modelled for me what it means to live beyond my excuses.

Those of you who gave feedback on my early manuscript: Elizabeth Hoa Nguyễn, Nanette O'Neal, Mark Heywood, Terry Stafford, Joan Turley, and Martyn Wood.

Last but not least—my Senior Pastors, Sean and Lynda Stanton: I stand among the grateful multitude, impacted by your decades of faithfulness to Jesus. I believe your best years are still in front of you.

ABOUT THE AUTHOR

Stuart Lamont's life mission is to meet people in the valley, and take them up the mountain. He is passionate about helping others build an authentic relationship with God.

He uses lessons learned during his own "valley" experiences to help encourage others to strive for greater spiritual maturity.

He also gained insight into other cultures as an educator in Seoul, South Korea and as a student in Japan. He graduated from the Australian National University with an extended major in the Japanese language.

Stuart is a Christ-follower, musician, husband, father, and occasional tech enthusiast. He and his wife Cherie live in Canberra, Australia, together with their two children.

Connect with Stuart at his website: *StuartLamont.me*.

NOTES

Foreword
1. Ephesians 6:12 NIV

Introduction
2. 1 Kings 18:1-40 NIV
3. 2 Peter 3:8 NIV
4. Luke 6:46-49 NIV
5. John 15:5-6 NIV
6. Matthew 24:12 NIV
7. 2 Corinthians 5:17 NIV
8. John 17:16 NIV
9. Nehemiah 2:19 NIV

Chapter 1 – The Wake-Up Call
10. John 10:9 NIV
11. 2 Peter 3:8 NIV
12. Philippians 3:20 NIV
13. Nehemiah 1:3 NIV
14. Nehemiah 1:4 NIV
15. 1 Peter 5:6 NIV
16. Nehemiah 1:5-6,10-11 NIV
17. J.P. Moreland and Klaus Issler, *In search of a confident faith: overcoming barriers to trusting in God* (Downer's Grove, Illinois: Inter-Varsity Press, USA, 2008), 17.

Chapter 2 – What Do You Want?
18. Nehemiah 2:1-3 NIV
19. Nehemiah 2:4 NIV

20. Nehemiah 2:4-5 NIV
21. John 1:1 NIV
22. John 5:1-5 NIV
23. John 5:6 NIV
24. Proverbs 13:12 NIV
25. Proverbs 18:14 NIV
26. John 5:6-9 NIV
27. Revelation 12:11 NIV
28. Psalm 77:11 NIV
29. Romans 8:31 NIV
30. 2 Timothy 2:4 NIV

Chapter 3 – The Cycle of Spiritual Growth
31. Romans 5:2-4 NIV
32. Hebrews 5:8 NIV
33. Isaiah 64:8 NIV
34. 1 Peter 5:6 NIV
35. Galatians 6:9 NIV
36. Romans 5:5 NIV
37. Philippians 2:12-13 NIV

Chapter 4 – Why Grow?
38. 2 Peter 1:3-9 NIV
39. John 1:42 NIV
40. John 21:15-19 NIV
41. 2 Timothy 4:2 NIV
42. 1 Peter 5:7 NIV
43. Romans 12:1-2 NIV
44. Ecclesiastes 12:1 NIV
45. Luke 23:42-43 NIV
46. Matthew 25:1-13
47. https://alpha.org/
48. Proverbs 14:8 NIV
49. Psalm 121:4 NIV

Chapter 5 – The Paradigm Shift
50. 2 Corinthians 5:21 NIV; Ephesians 2:7 NIV
51. Romans 5:2 NIV
52. Hebrews 5:11-14 MSG
53. Hebrews 6:1-3 MSG
54. Genesis 15:3-6 NIV
55. Romans 4:2-4 NIV
56. Genesis 12:11-15 NIV
57. Galatians 4:21-31 NIV
58. Romans 12:1-2 MSG

Chapter 6 – Are You a Good Person?
59. Romans 3:23 NIV
60. Matthew 16:16-17 ESV
61. Acts 4:12
62. Romans 5:2 NIV
63. 2 Corinthians 5:21 MSG
64. John 3:16 NIV
65. Romans 10:9 NIV
66. Genesis 20:2 NIV
67. Genesis 27:35-36 NIV
68. Exodus 2:12 NIV
69. 2 Samuel 12:1-10 NIV
70. John 5:24 ESV
71. James 2:14-17 NIV
72. Matthew 17:1-4 NIV
73. Matthew 17:5 NIV
74. Matthew 17:5-7 NIV

Chapter 7 – Sonship
75. Romans 8:14-17 NIV
76. Luke 11:11-13 NIV
77. Jeremiah 29:11 NIV
78. Psalm 27:10 NIV
79. Psalm 139:4 NIV

NOTES

80. James 1:17 NIV
81. 1 Corinthians 10:13-14 NIV
82. 2 Corinthians 5:17 NIV
83. Ephesians 2:10 NIV
84. Luke 15:24 NIV
85. Matthew 3:13-17 NIV
86. Romans 8:29 NIV
87. Philippians 2:15

Chapter 8 – God is With You
88. Hebrews 13:5 NIV
89. Matthew 28:20 NIV
90. John 3:16 NIV
91. Romans 8:11 NIV
92. Romans 2:4 NIV
93. Luke 11:11-13 NIV
94. Isaiah 30:21 NIV
95. Revelation 3:20 NIV
96. Genesis 4:7 NIV
97. Genesis 3:1-19 NIV
98. 1 Thessalonians 5:21 NIV; 2 Corinthians 10:5 NIV
99. Revelation 12:20 NIV
100. Romans 8:1 NIV
101. Romans 4:25-5:1 NIV
102. James 1:17 NIV
103. John 14:9 NIV
104. 2 Timothy 1:7
105. John 14:25-26 NIV
106. John 10:27 NIV
107. Romans 5:5 NIV
108. Romans 8:26-27 NIV
109. 1 Samuel 30:6 NIV
110. John 3:8 NIV
111. Matthew 7:13-14 NIV

Chapter 9 – Shared Success
112. Hebrews 13:5 NIV
113. James 1:17 NIV
114. Numbers 23:19 NIV
115. Romans 2:4
116. Ephesians 4:26 NIV
117. Romans 5:8 NIV
118. Matthew 6:15 NLT
119. Genesis 2:18 NIV
120. Hebrews 10:25 NIV
121. Nehemiah 2:11-19 NIV
122. John 2:24 NIV
123. Nehemiah 2:19 NIV
124. Nehemiah 2:5-9 NIV
125. Nehemiah 2:20 NIV
126. Exodus 6:28-7:5 NIV
127. 1 Samuel 30:6 KJV
128. Psalm 27:10 NIV
129. Matthew 7:12 NIV
130. 2 Timothy 1:7 ESV

Chapter 10 – Let God PICK
131. Proverbs 27:9 NIV
132. 2 Corinthians 2:15-16 NIV
133. Proverbs 27:6 NIV
134. 1 Corinthians 12:16 NIV
135. John 13:34-35 NIV
136. John 15:13 NIV
137. 2 Corinthians 5:16 NIV
138. 2 Corinthians 5:17 NIV
139. Proverbs 27:17 NIV
140. Luke 9:50 NIV
141. Romans 2:4 NIV
142. Romans 5:8 NIV
143. Matthew 12:43-45 NIV

Chapter 11 – For Different Seasons and Different Reasons
144. Ecclesiastes 3:1 ESV
145. Romans 12:18 NIV
146. Hebrews 13:8 NIV
147. Numbers 23:19 NIV
148. 1 John 3:14 NIV
149. Hebrews 13:5 NIV
150. Psalm 73:26 NIV
151. Exodus 33:11
152. Ephesians 1:11 MSG
153. John 12:24 NIV
154. Acts 20:36-38 NIV
155. Psalm 139:16 NIV

Chapter 12 – Don't Be a Stranger
156. Ephesians 2:4-7 NIV
157. Matthew 10:28 NIV
158. 2 Timothy 1:12 NIV
159. Matthew 22:15-16 ESV [emphasis mine]
160. *The Value Thinline Edition, English Standard Version® (ESV®)* (Wheaton, Illinois: Crossway, USA, 2002), 827, Footnote 5 [Matthew 22:16].
161. Matthew 16:21-23 NIV
162. Galatians 1:10 NIV
163. John 1:43-48 NIV

Chapter 13 – Chasing Fantasy
164. Isaiah 55:8-9 NIV
165. Romans 8:28 NIV
166. Psalm 8:3-4 NIV
167. Psalm 51:5 NIV
168. Ephesians 2:1-3
169. Ephesians 2:8-10 NIV
170. James 4:14 NLT
171. Jeremiah 28:1-17 NIV
172. Jeremiah 28:13-16 NIV
173. Luke 17:1 NIV
174. Luke 9:57-58 NIV
175. Matthew 9:4 NIV
176. 1 Peter 1:7 NIV
177. Jeremiah 29:10-12 NIV
178. Ecclesiastes 11:4 NIV
179. Psalm 37:1-2 NIV
180. Psalm 37:3 NIV
181. Proverbs 28:19 NIV
182. Psalm 37:4 NIV
183. James 4:8 NIV
184. 2 Corinthians 12:9 NIV
185. Psalm 18:19 NIV

Chapter 14 – Zeal Without Knowledge
186. Nehemiah 4:6-10 NIV
187. Matthew 13:18-23 NIV
188. Exodus 33:11 NIV
189. Genesis 1:26-27 NIV
190. 2 Corinthians 10:5 NIV
191. Proverbs 9:10 NIV
192. Ephesians 2:6 NIV
193. Proverbs 19:23 NIV
194. Acts 22:1-21 NIV
195. Romans 10:1-4 NIV
196. Proverbs 19:2 NIV
197. 1 Kings 19:11-12 NIV
198. 1 Thessalonians 5:21 NIV
199. 2 Timothy 3:16-17 NIV
200. Romans 12:1 MSG

NOTES

Chapter 15 – The Unsealed Letter
201. Ephesians 6:12 NIV
202. John 14:29-31 NIV
203. John 16:33 NIV
204. Nehemiah 6:1 NIV
205. Nehemiah 6:5-7 NIV
206. James 4:7 NIV
207. Nehemiah 6:9 NIV
208. Psalm 134:2 NIV
209. Psalm 18:33-34 NIV
210. James 4:7-8 NIV
211. 2 Timothy 2:1-4 NIV
212. Psalm 123:2 NIV
213. 2 Kings 6:16 NIV
214. 2 Kings 6:17 NIV
215. Psalm 116:7-9 NIV
216. Hebrews 4:9-11 NIV
217. Isaiah 40:29-31 NIV
218. Matthew 4:3 NIV
219. Hebrews 10:19-23 NIV
220. Psalm 40:3 NIV
221. Exodus 17:11 NIV
222. Exodus 17:12-13 NIV
223. Psalm 16:11 NIV
224. Nehemiah 8:10 NIV
225. Judges 7:9-15 NIV

Chapter 16 – The City Gates
226. Proverbs 4:23 NIV
227. Nehemiah 6:1 NIV
228. Nehemiah 1:3 NIV
229. Isaiah 30:21 NIV
230. Matthew 28:18 NIV
231. 1 Kings 4:30
232. 1 Kings 11:1-13
233. Matthew 12:34
234. 1 Thessalonians 5:21
235. John 10:27 NIV
236. Romans 12:1-2 NIV
237. 1 Samuel 17:40,49 NIV

Conclusion – Our Enemy Trembles
238. Nehemiah 6:15-16 NIV

Appendix – Believing in Jesus
239. Romans 10:9-10 MSG
240. 2 Corinthians 5:17
241. John 5:24 ESV

www.ingramcontent.com/pod-product-compliance
Lightning Source LLC
LaVergne TN
LVHW011822060526
838200LV00053B/3872